LADY IN WHITE

Lady in White

The Killing of John de Saulles
by His Ex-Wife Blanca Errázuriz

Denise B. Tanaka

Sasoriza Books
San Jose, California

Copyright ©2017 by Denise B. Tanaka

ISBN: 978-1-946055-04-0

SASORIZA BOOKS
P.O. Box 9033
San Jose, CA 95157
www.sasorizabooks.com
https://www.facebook.com/SasorizaBooks/
www.jackdesaulles.blogspot.com

Cover design by Elina Tanaka
Blanca de Saulles in court, on trial for murder

Contents

Acknowledgments

The Internet could only take me so far before I had to dig into sources the old-fashioned way. I gained access to the rare documents and special collections archives of Yale University, the Cecil H. Green Library at Stanford University, the Abraham Lincoln Presidential Library, and the Nassau County Court in New York. My gratitude goes to Eleanor Nothelfer at Lehigh University, to Jonathan Eaker at the Library of Congress Photographs Division, to Lynne Crowley at the Larchmont Historical Society, and to Ann Southwell at the Albert & Shirley Small Special Collections Library of the University of Virginia for their generous assistance.

A very special thanks goes to Suzette Davidson for editorial review, to Shael and Judy Hawman for encouragement, and to my family for their unwavering love and support.

A quick note on Spanish-style names:

Generally, a person's given name is followed by a composite of two family names/surnames. The first surname carries down from the father's family, and the second is from the mother's paternal line. If a man's first wife dies, the children of his second wife will often have a different second (maternal) surname. For example, Federico Errázuriz Zañartu and Maximiano Errázuriz Valdivieso are half-brothers with the same father but two different mothers.

A man's name will not change throughout his life, but when a woman marries, she may drop the maternal surname and substitute the surname of her husband linked by the prefix "de." For example, Blanca Vergara Alvarez changed her name to Blanca Vergara de Errázuriz upon her marriage to Guillermo Errázuriz Urmeneta.

Gridiron Hero

If you are gaining at a certain place,
do not be afraid to work it for all it is worth,
until you cannot gain there any more,
then it will be time to try another play.

JOHN LONGER DE SAULLES

John Longer de Saulles—or "Jack" to his friends—grew up in Pennsylvania before the turn of the 20th Century, at a time when the rural countryside experienced its dramatic transformation with the developing steel industry. His father, a native of New Orleans and a Civil War veteran, worked as superintendent of the New Jersey Zinc Company in Bethlehem, Pennsylvania. His older brother Charles was a very studious civil engineer. His second older brother Arthur Percy died at age 21 after complications from a surgery, and another brother died within a day of being born. He grew up with the companionship of two sisters Georgiana Armide and Caroline Belmont de Saulles.

John had a youthful zest for life and a jolly personality who made friends easily. Everyone knew him as a handsome, popular guy, charming and fun to be around. He stood a bit shorter than average, at 5 feet 8 inches tall, and like his father had sparkling blue eyes and dark brown hair. He was a bachelor at heart and a bit of a Peter Pan, delaying marriage until his early thirties.

"When I was a little shaver, back in 1889, I lived at South Bethlehem, Pa," he later reminisced in *Football Days*, a collection of mini-memoirs from the greatest names in sports at the time. "Paul Dashiell and Mathew McClung, who were then playing football at Lehigh University, took an interest in me. Paul Dashiell took me to the first football game I ever saw. Dibby McClung gave me one of the old practice balls of the Lehigh team. This was the first football I ever had in my hands. For weeks afterwards that football was my nightly companion in bed. These two Lehigh stars have always been my football heroes..."[1]

At the turn of the century, American football was in its infancy as a sport. Walter Camp adapted the game from the English rugby and developed most of the techniques we know today. In those days, football was part of the college athletic curriculum. Before cities sponsored professional teams, the sports departments of universities captured the public's interest. National newspapers reported on the tackles and touchdowns of college games. Rivalries built up friendly tension between the Ivy League schools of Yale, Harvard, and Princeton, and every college in the country from Stanford to Cornell assembled their own teams. Stadiums at university athletic fields packed in thousands of cheering spectators who politely waved the colored banners of their favorite schools; the fans had not yet invented the beer-dispensing helmet, body paint, or the oversized foam Number One finger. In those days, there was fleeting fame and local glory but no fortune to be made.

John began his studies at Yale University in the Scientific School aspiring to be a civil engineer like his father and older brother. Rocks and minerals did not hold his interest. He broke with family tradition and chose a transfer to the Law School, but it was on the athletic field—as star quarterback of the varsity football team—where he made a name for himself. Restless and sociable, team sports provided an outlet for his energies. Quickly emerging from his older brother's shadow (Charlie had played football at Yale, too), he earned a reputation as a gridiron hero who could do amazing things on the field.

Fig. 1 - John L. de Saulles in Yale University football uniform (circa 1901)

John became one of America's first nationally famous football stars. His team played consistently well and enjoyed victory as much from strategy as from athleticism. Of course the coach was the driving force and the team was effectively managed by the professors in Yale's athletic department. Once the team got onto the field, though, the quarterback took command. A football rules manual edited by Walter Camp in 1902 gives a review of the previous season and names John de Saulles as one of the top quarterbacks in the country for his first-class "...handling of the ball, catching of punts, running back and tackling."[2] A bit shorter than average, wiry and agile, John slipped past the reach of brawny linebackers. If tackled, he hopped to his feet and kept going. For John, football was not just a game; it became his philosophy of life. Losses were temporary setbacks to overcome, and any goal could be reached if one kept pushing forward... until the clock ran out.

He recalled an anecdote in *Football Days*, "Billy Bull and I have often discussed the fact that when an attempt for a goal from the field failed, one of the players of the opposing side always touched the ball back of the goal line (thereby making it dead), and brought it out to the 25-yard line to kick. Of course, the ball is never dead until it is touched down. It was in the fall of 1902 [sic][3] when we were playing West Point. In the latter part of the second half of that game, with the score 6 to 6, Charlie Daly attempted a field goal, which was unsuccessful. What Billy Bull and I had discussed many times came into my mind like a flash. I picked the ball up and walked out with it as if it had been touched back of the goal. When I passed the 25-yard line, walking along casually,

Bucky Vail, who was the referee, yelled to me to stop. I walked over to him unconcerned and said: 'Bucky, old boy! This ball is not dead, because I did not touch it down. And I am going down the field with it.' By that time the West Point men had taken their positions in order to receive the kick from the 25-yard line. While I was still walking down the field, in order to pass all the West Point men, before making my dash for a certain touchdown, it struck Bucky Vail that I was right, and he yelled out at the top of his voice. 'The ball is not dead. It is free.' Whereupon the West Point men started after me. An Army man tackled me on their 25-yard line, after I had taken the ball down the field for nearly a touchdown. I have often turned over in my bed at night since that time, cursing the action of Referee Vail. If he had not interfered with my play I would have walked down the field for a touchdown and victory for Yale. The final score remained 6 to 6."

At one notable game, Yale defeated Princeton with a score of 12 to zero and Princeton never managed to get any closer than Yale's 30-yard line. The Sunday edition of the *Washington Times*, November 17, 1901, credits the quarterback John de Saulles with almost single-handedly winning the game. In one play he made a catch at the far end of the field and, dodging all attempts to tackle him, sprinted for a gain of 25 yards. He made several spectacular punts and choreographed strategies that obliterated the Princeton team.

However, the Yale team's thrill at this victory gave them a little too much confidence. They soon felt the agony of defeat the following week at a game against Harvard. The newspapers had built up high expectations for Yale's performance but the team could not accomplish a single touchdown. A strong northwest wind blew snow flurries from a dark gray sky like an omen of doom. Crushed by a score of 22 to zero[4], the Yale men staggered off the field wondering where it all went wrong.

John suffered an injury during this Harvard game when he took a hard knock to the head. A fellow named Marshall, from the opposing team, intercepted one of John's punts and started running the length of the field. John dashed straight for him to block the Harvard man from scoring. Running full tilt, he attempted a flying tackle. Marshall leaped to dodge. Either his knee or his shoe collided with John's skull. In those days, the quarterback did not wear any kind of protective headgear; only the linebackers had leather caps. John was knocked out, cold, and had to be carried away on a stretcher.

This serious head injury panicked his family. Only five years earlier they had buried John's other brother, Arthur Percy, who had been at the same age when a sudden illness struck him down. To see John laid out pale in a hospital bed, his bruised head wrapped in bandages, aroused a terror of losing him too. I doubt if John shared his father's concern for his personal safety, or if he did, he would not want to admit it. What twenty-three year old gives a passing thought to his own mortality?

Well wishes poured in to Boston's Massachusetts General Hospital from both teams. School rivalries crumbled away as every man who had been in the game—crimson and blue uniforms side by side—offered their concern for the "plucky" efforts of the little Yale quarterback.[5] Doctors gave frequent updates to the newspapermen clamoring in the lobby. John's condition stabilized that night but the physicians recommended keeping him in the hospital an extra day to avoid exposing him to a powerful snow storm wailing at the dark windows.

As a result of this injury, John put aside what he loved most. For his own safety and his family's peace of mind, he never competed in another football game.

Despite the pain and threat of death, John had no regrets and years later would look back on the Harvard game with pride. He wrote in *Football Days*, published the year before his murder, "I have often thought of the painful hours I would have suffered had I missed the two open field chances in the disastrous game at Cambridge... when Yale was beaten 23 to 0. On two different occasions in that game a Harvard runner with interference had passed the whole Yale team. I was the only Yale man between the Harvard man and a touchdown. The supreme satisfaction I had in nailing both of those runners is one of the most pleasant recollections of my football career."

Spring brought the baseball season, and John de Saulles found a new place on Yale's varsity baseball team. He finished out his last year of college as a second baseman. A group photograph in the *New York Daily Tribune,* April 7, 1902, shows him smiling with the rest of the team, a cap and catcher's mitt in his hands, but one has to wonder if he missed the football field. John had an active, restless spirit that was always on the move; playing in-field or guarding second base seems like too much of standing still.

To celebrate graduation, John took a holiday trip to England in August 1902 with his buddy Coleman Carnegie, the nephew of Andrew Carnegie the multi-millionaire. "Coley" Carnegie, as he was known to his friends, was one of nine children born to Andrew's less famous brother Thomas who had died of illness in 1886 when Coley was just six years old. For all his material wealth, the legendary tycoon himself did not have a male heir to his name; he only had a daughter. Rumors circulated in the newspapers that Coley was Andrew Carnegie's favorite nephew out of the bunch, with promise to become the next Lord of Skibo (the family's ancestral lands in Scotland) but on one condition. "'If Coley will straighten up,' Andrew Carnegie announced to the newspapers, 'I will take him to Scotland and make a real laird of the boy.'"[6] The young man's efforts to go sober were reported in the newspapers, which reveals what a party animal Coley Carnegie must have been. In those days, there was no concept of celebrity rehab.

Imagine the two college graduates on a bachelor's holiday, guzzling warm black beer in Scottish pubs or daring each other to eat *haggis* and laughing at each other when they gagged. Life seemed full of limitless promise. Their families expected great things from these boys and their own dreams soared even higher. The two soon returned to North America to nurse their hangovers. They shared an apartment in New York City, and Coley Carnegie made an attempt to earn his uncle's respect by taking a job at Bloodgood & Company a real estate firm.[7]

John had graduated with a degree in law, but for his first job in the fall of 1902 he and two other Yale alumni spent a season coaching the Cavaliers football team at the University of Virginia. His students affectionately called him "Kid" de Saulles, a nickname that would stick with him the rest of his life. The *Corks and Curls* yearbook of 1903 honored their visiting coaches who "came as strangers out of the North... living with us for a season, breaking our bread, sharing our hopes and stimulating our ambitions." Of the three coaches Wesley Abbott, B.C. Chamberlain, and John de Saulles, the yearbook made a special mention of the Kid, "...knowing few, was known by all, tender in words but fierce in action, possessing all the graces of a gentleman, by heredity, by instinct, and by acquirement."[8]

The University of Virginia presented John with a loving cup trophy at an Easter banquet the following spring to publicly thank him for his valuable services in coaching the team to victory. Invited to the banquet were John's father Major Arthur de Saulles, his Yale baseball teammate Arthur Barnwell, and his good buddy Coley Carnegie. The local newspaper *The Times Dispatch* reported that John donated his entire salary to the General Athletic Association and would not accept a penny. The *Corks and Curls* yearbook confirms that John "not only absolutely declined any remuneration for his time or services, but was involved in considerable financial outlay." In other words, he dedicated himself to coaching the team of a rival school through an entire season simply for the love of the game.

John de Saulles wrote an open letter to Dr. William A. Lambeth, an esteemed professor and medical advisor at the University of Virginia athletics department, reprinted in the local newspaper. "The work the men did for me on the team was most gratifying and, considering we had but two old men to build on, I consider our record a magnificent one. You have no idea how much it meant to us to beat the Indians. Everybody I have met since I left Charlottesville has congratulated me upon Virginia's success this fall, and I can tell you I have met not a few people since I last saw you. On the side line of the navy-yard game alone I had at least ten or twelve men away up in the football world, including Walter Camp and Paul Dashiell, come up to me and offer their congratulations to Virginia."[9]

Fig. 2 - a Yale football team in action

As a side project, John wrote a chapter for one of Walter Camp's many publications, *How to Play Football: A Primer on the Modern College Game with Tactics Brought Down to Date*, published in 1904 by Spalding's sports equipment company. This book followed on the 1902 edition, *Rules of Football*, that established a winning format of instructional essays combined with a mail order catalog. First a heroic icon like Walter Camp explains theory and techniques in clear textbook style. Then, the catalog offers readers the necessary equipment to start a team in their own hometown.

John's 10-page essay "How to Play Quarterback" in the 1904 edition is illustrated with rare (posed) photographs of The Kid in action demonstrating some basic moves. Before the days of

11

television, most people outside of college campuses had never witnessed a football game. This book spread the knowledge to a general audience. "The quarter-back of today in his relationship to a foot ball team must be a good general, must have an abundant supply of foot ball nerve, almost twice as much physical endurance as any other man on the team, and an ability to handle the ball cleanly and swiftly."[10] He gives advice to novice players, "Handling punts well will only come with long practice, but it is essential that a man handling a punt in the backfield should keep both his eye and mind firmly fixed on the ball, and pay no attention to the tacklers coming down the field, until after the ball is caught."[11] He gives detailed explanations of maneuvers and positioning, "As in Fig. 1, Quarter directly behind centre, hands spread out in most natural way to receive ball, knees bent in an easy position with feel well separated, so that backs can see the ball, as in Fig. 2. Neither foot should be advanced, but both should be in a straight line parallel to the rush line."[12]

Fig. 3 - John L. de Saulles demonstrating football quarterback techniques

His writing voice gives a rare insight as to what sort of advice he gave as a coach. "Receiving the ball properly from the centre is a most important factor. The quarter cannot practice this too much with his centre, in order that he need not worry about how high or how low the ball will come from the centre, or how fast or how slow, but may know that he will receive it with a uniform speed and at one height constantly, thereby feeling that he has only to consider how quickly he may get the ball to the runner. The quarter should coach his centre from time to time, letting him know when the ball is not coming exactly right, and showing him just where and at what speed he wants it. In case of a fumble between centre and quarter (and this should be stamped on every quarter's heart), *drop on the ball, don't try to pick it up*." [13]

It was an honor for John to contribute to this volume. There were no other books on football being published at the time. The game was heavily criticized in those days for its brutal physicality and high injury rate, and there was a real danger of it being banned outright. Walter Camp played a leading role in giving public legitimacy to the game by his leadership in the American Football Rules Committee that established and enforced the rules of good sportsmanship. He helped to establish the National Collegiate Athletic Association and with President Wilson's endorsement during the First World War, he supervised the physical training of our armed forces.[14] Until his death in 1925, Camp remained active in promoting the sport and is credited as the one who saved football from extinction. He built the game of football into America's favorite pastime with support from celebrity colleagues like John de Saulles.

Fig. 4 - portrait of Walter Camp in football gear

John's philosophy of generalship not only applies to football but to how he conducted his life. "In the game, be deliberate in initiating the play, but when once started go ahead with determination and dash. At all times observe closely the opposing line, and if you discover an opponent playing too wide send a player there.... If you are gaining at a certain place, do not be afraid to work it for all it is worth, until you cannot gain there any more, then it will be time to try another play... Trick plays should be avoided inside your own forty-yard line, unless time is nearly up and you must score or lose the game."[15]

Blanquita

...Something in me keeps on crying.

BLANCA ERRÁZURIZ VERGARA

On the other side of the world from where John de Saulles enjoyed fame as a football quarterback, Blanca Errázuriz Vergara led a sheltered childhood in Chile. Her prestigious ancestry on both her father's and her mother's side had earned their elite status as presidents, senators, archbishops, industrialists, and war heroes. Their genealogy is well documented and their biographies appear in numerous history books.

The Errázuriz winery continues to operate in the Aconcagua Valley north of Santiago. Founded by Blanca's grandfather Maximiano, the climate and composition of the soil—comparable to the Napa Valley in northern California—is ideal for cultivating wine grapes. Frosty-topped mountain ranges surround lush green hills watered by indigo streams. At the time, most of the other prestigious families were planting vineyards in the outskirts of the capital city, but Maximiano followed his own pioneering vision by settling farther away. He dedicated his vineyards with the motto, "*de la major tierra, el major vino,*" meaning, "from the best land, the best wine."

At the turn of the century, Chile experienced a boom of industrial development and foreign investors flocked to this

17

shoreline nation to exploit the natural resources. The nearby city of Valparaiso quickly grew into a bustling metropolis, but Blanca's hometown Viña del Mar (founded and developed by her maternal grandfather José Francisco Vergara Echevers) remained a haven of serenity, an oasis of clear, floral-scented air. Whenever she traveled throughout her life, Blanca always yearned to return to these crystal blue waters and white sand beaches.

When Blanca was only three years old, her father Guillermo Errázuriz contracted tuberculosis and died. He had been a lawyer who administered the mining interests of his family in various territories, which meant he often traveled away from home. He chose to live in the seaside town of Viña del Mar for the convenience of the seaport so he could easily depart for Lebu or Coquimbo or take a steamship to Europe when the need required it. Guillermo Errázuriz died at age 31 in Paris, France on the 18th of August 1897,[16] leaving behind his widow and five children. Blanca never had a chance to know her father, and her widowed mother Doña Blanca Vergara de Errázuriz never remarried.

Her older brother Hugo died at age 11 by accidentally falling off a horse. Blanca was about seven years old, too young to have anything but childish memories of him. To cope with her grief, the widow Doña Blanca established an elementary school in

1903 dedicated to Hugo's memory. The parochial school Escuela Hugo Errázuriz No. 24, affiliated with the nearby *Nuestra Señora de los Dolores* village church, is still active and celebrated its centennial in 2003.

Her elder sister Manuela took vows to become a Poor Clare nun. She entered a cloistered convent *Nuestra Senora de la Victoria* in Santiago, Chile and remained isolated from the family for the rest of her life. For all practical purposes, by devoting her life to God alone, Manuela became inaccessible as if she had already entered Heaven while on Earth.

These losses in her early childhood left Blanca with only two siblings in the household. Her sister Amalia and her brother Guillermo ("Billy") formed a trio as intimate as the Three Musketeers, close in age, constant companions and playmates, and later as adults unconditionally supportive and dependent on each other.

At a young age, Blanca suffered a head injury while playing with her sister Amalia. When running and playing tag around the mansion's grounds, Blanca tripped and fell against one of the stone andirons of the balcony. She was bed-ridden and delirious for several days. So soon after losing Hugo in an accident, her mother trembled to the core. Doña Blanca lit candles at the church and prayed to the Holy Virgin Mary and all the saints in Heaven to bring her daughter through this crisis. Blanca recovered

19

but, as her sister later said on the witness stand, she was never quite the same.

Fig. 5 - Blanca Errázuriz Vergara (Mrs. John de Saulles)

Blanca was sent away to England to be educated at a Sacred Heart convent school. Her etiquette was polished into an aristocratic poise. Here she learned the self-control she would later display at her murder trial. I imagine that she endured getting her knuckles whacked by stern nuns, kneeling to recite the rosary, whispering confessions in the dark to an old priest through a screen window, and memorizing the catalog of sins in her catechism studies. She learned proper English diction and picked up slang phrases, criticizing undesirable things as "just beastly." She wore corsets, lace gowns and fashionable hats, but she would always feel out of place as a Hispanic girl in a Caucasian world. Her natural desire to fit in with her blue-eyed blonde classmates was rejected when they perceived her dark complexion as exotic and alien. To survive, she would need to suppress and restrain her frustration. If teased or ridiculed, she did not dare fight back. Chile was a land of volcanoes, and Blanca herself became one. Years later, when interviewed just after her acquittal for John's murder, reporters asked Blanca how she had preserved her "mask of calm and indifference" throughout the ordeal of the trial. She replied, "I schooled myself to it beforehand. I knew that psychologists and every one else would be watching me, and I steeled myself to hold my expression. It was very hard, but one can do what one has to do."[17]

While she was away at school in England, an earthquake slammed the city of Valparaiso, Chile at a few minutes before 8:00 PM on Thursday, August 16, 1906. Recorded at a magnitude of 8.2, it was stronger than the San Francisco earthquake (7.8) of a few months before. Houses in the city crumbled. Electric lights went dark. Telephone and telegraph lines snapped. Bridges toppled. Railroad lines buckled. Fire bells rang throughout the city. A few blazes broke out, but a cold dark rain showered down and extinguished them. Crowds wailed and prayed in the streets. Masses huddled together and spent the night out of doors in the public squares and cracked brick avenues.

More than 80 aftershocks rattled the city overnight. When dawn of Friday morning illuminated the damage, the survivors could see that most of the city's buildings had been ruined or completely leveled. The local church of Our Lady of Sorrows (*Nuestra Señora de los Dolores*), originally built by Blanca's ancestors, was also destroyed and would later be rebuilt from the foundation. The grim task of counting the corpses and rescuing the injured consumed the next few weeks. It is estimated that almost 4,000 people died.

The captain of a steamship told the newspapers that, in his observation, the damage was far worse than what he had seen recently in San Francisco. The port of Valparaiso was the largest seaport on the Pacific Ocean, equal to the Golden Gate in the volume of shipping trade, and the economic loss was enormous. Not only was the city at the epicenter of the event, but villages and towns all around it suffered the impact. The towns of Limache, Quillota, and Viña del Mar were completely destroyed. Thousands of people were rendered homeless. To make matters worse, August is the winter season in the southern hemisphere. Cold winds and chilling rains tormented the people trying to sleep, wrapped in nothing but blankets, in the open air. Martial law took effect and authorities commanded the rationing of food supplies. After a week, a few trains got up and running to carry some of the refugees away to Santiago and to bring in donations from sympathetic nations around the world.

The 1906 earthquake also destroyed Blanca's family home. The mansion had been a luxurious two-story structure with a domed tower and a widow's walk on the roof. A full length veranda had an elegant stone balustrade where Blanca had struck her head as a child. Gabled windows and a covered wraparound porch had been shaded by tall palm trees. In an historic photograph, it is a gleaming white palace set against the darker backdrop of an old growth forest.[18] In a matter of minutes, it crumbled to its foundations.

Fig. 6 - her mother, Blanca Vergara de Errázuriz (circa 1910)

The widow Doña Blanca supervised the rebuilding of a more spectacular mansion on the site. She employed Ettore Petri, an Italian architect, to spend the next two years on the reconstruction. A contemporary photograph dedicated to the architect shows Doña Blanca in a lacy white dress posed like a queen, serene and ethereal. Her daughter Blanca would cherish this portrait of her mother and later bring it with her to the U.S.

The new Venetian style mansion known as Palacio Vergara is an imposing yet elegant structure fit for royalty. The silhouette is blocky and rectangular, but its harsh outline is softened by miter archways and trimmings of white stone sculpted to resemble fine Italian lace. Luxury antique furniture was shipped in directly from Europe. Tall narrow windows allowed plenty of sunlight to illuminate the collection of artwork that Doña Blanca displayed on the spacious interior walls. When she practiced on the grand piano, the glorious music of Mozart and Liszt resounded throughout the lofty rooms.

French architects landscaped the surrounding grounds of Quinta Vergara Park into beautiful gardens with a dazzling variety of exotic trees and shrubs imported from the Orient and Europe, something like a Versailles of South America.

Fig. 7 - Palacio Vergara, Viña del Mar, Chile
before the 1906 earthquake (top) and present day (bottom)

Tea trees from China, coffee trees from Brazil, eucalyptus from Australia, geranium blossoms and palm trees, herbal maté, Lebanon cedars, California sequoias, and many native Chilean species thrived beyond his lifetime. Doña Blanca took great pride in preserving her grandfather's legacy of fragrance and greenery. Today the mansion is a school of fine arts and a museum, but in 1908, Doña Blanca intended the palace to be the family home and capitol building of an enduring dynasty that was fated never to be.

Blanca returned from the English school at age 14, blossoming into a young lady.[19] The home she had known before the earthquake was transformed into a gleaming marble palace with life-sized sculptures of lions reclining at the entrance gate. Grecian statues of modestly draped goddesses stood eternally silent in the flower gardens.

The town of Viña del Mar had recovered from the earthquake, rebuilt, and made itself into a new beautiful being like Blanca herself on the verge of womanhood. Steam trains on newly laid tracks brought travelers from afar. Automobiles rolled on paved streets. On a clear day, she could hear the church bells of *Nuestra Señora de los Dolores* in the city's central plaza.

A charming young debutante, Blanca entertained suitable young men in society circles at a polite distance. She fully expected to marry a nice Chilean boy and raise a family basking on these sunny seaside beaches, breathing the perfume of eucalyptus trees. Never did she imagine herself as the wife of a North American living in a steel-refining Pennsylvania town.

Skyscraper

The rich are different from us.

F. SCOTT FITZGERALD
AUTHOR

Now in his late twenties, John de Saulles left the world of sports behind. He settled in New York City and changed careers to something less physical. Putting his people skills and law degree to good use, he entered the field of real estate investments. Coley Carnegie introduced him into the firm of Bloodgood & Company where John's gregarious personality thrived in the art of salesmanship. Within a few years, as Coley's addictions spiraled his life out of control, John advanced to hold a prominent place in the renamed firm of Bloodgood, de Saulles & Talbot dealing with luxury residential and commercial properties[20]. He changed to wearing stylish suits instead of a football jersey, but in his heart it was still about the game; every signed lease felt like a touchdown.

At the turn of the century, New York City boomed with development and the Industrial Revolution reaped the profits of new technology. Inventions changed the quality of everyday life. The telephone, the typewriter, electric light bulbs, and the automobile laid the foundation for the modern world of today. Factory-made commodities replaced hand-made crafts. No longer did housewives toil at spinning their own cloth or weaving their own baskets. Sears Roebuck and Montgomery Ward department stores produced mail order catalogs where the average person could purchase almost any desired item (clothes, furniture, household appliances, pharmaceuticals, or rifles and revolvers) to be delivered to their doorstep. Automobiles, bicycles, and trolleys started to replace horse drawn carriages. Everything moved faster. One could cross the Atlantic Ocean on a steel steamship in only five days! The Brooklyn Bridge gleamed brand new. Office buildings of steel and brick soared taller every year, on the verge of being called skyscrapers.

John's trophy accomplishment was his investment in the Nassau Hotel on the boardwalk of Long Beach, New York. This spectacular hotel would replace an old-style resort lodge and soon attracted thousands of city tourists to a once-deserted beach.

The original Long Beach Hotel since the early 1880s had occupied a quiet stretch of sand on the southern shore of Long Island, in the undeveloped suburbs east of New York City limits. The broad wooden building with its gabled windows and wraparound porch offered a restful getaway for wealthy clientele who had leisure time to enjoy the sun and the sea. The lodge and its twenty-five rustic cottages were often vacant and fell into bankruptcy. Offered for sale to the city of New York, the property was purchased instead in 1906 by the Long Beach Improvement Company that had the goal of transforming the area into another

Atlantic City getaway destination. Plans began for demolishing the outdated wooden structure to replace it with a modern steel and brick building.

Before demolition began, a fire destroyed the Long Beach Hotel in the early morning hours of July 29, 1907 at a total loss of the property but, remarkably, no loss of life. Over a thousand guests—including John de Saulles[21]—and the hotel's support staff escaped with their lives that day. An easterly wind held the flames to one corner of the structure just long enough for the sleeping guests to jump out of bed. A few injuries resulted when panicked vacationers hurled their heavy luggage and steamer trunks from second-story windows onto the people below. A couple others leaped out of windows and suffered broken legs. Senator McCarren and former Senator Reynolds, on-site representatives of the Long Beach Improvement Company, personally assisted in the rescue efforts. A bucket brigade formed using sea water to fight the flames. After several hours, the fire was at last controlled.

Standing in the charred ashes, Senator Reynolds boldly declared that the company would immediately begin construction of a new hotel. Lumber arrived for the new boardwalk on Long Beach and work began in the fall of 1907. Briefly, they experimented with using elephants to demolish ruined cottages and haul lumber. Borrowed from an animal show in Coney Island, the elephants did not perform well in the frigid temperatures. Old-fashioned human laborers were brought in to finish the job.

The newly constructed Nassau Hotel showcased a Spanish Renaissance style conceived by architects Lewis R. Kaufman and B.E. Stern. Three hundred rooms enjoyed piped running water. A rooftop garden and an orchestra ballroom with crystal chandeliers provided venues for guests to dine on local seafood and waltz the night away. The exterior decorations displayed warm earth tones of terra cotta and brick with varicolored faience. A gigantic fireplace made of caen stone, imported from France, dominated the interior foyer.[22] On its opening day in June 1909, the Nassau Hotel crowned a large section of the two-mile boardwalk where New York's elite could enjoy the pleasures of sunshine and polite games at the seaside.

While playing the real estate game, John cultivated a variety of new friendships. He gravitated toward men with a restless spirit like his own. John entered a business partnership with Paul J. Rainey, millionaire playboy and world explorer. Rainey gained fame as an African lion hunter and once lassoed a polar bear cowboy style that he donated to the Bronx zoo. Later he would produce several true-life adventure films with himself as the star. Rainey created a personal hunting retreat in Tennessee. The Tippah Lodge was extravagant and stylish with paved roads, an indoor swimming pool, a billiards room decorated with big game trophies, and a brick barn equipped to stable 50 polo ponies. Bold, charismatic, fearless and unstoppable, Rainey was the sort of daredevil that John de Saulles admired. Together they invested in the construction of a new steel pier at the far end of the Long Beach boardwalk and a casino entertainment center to rival Coney Island and Atlantic City.[23] John played his life like a football game, always looking ahead to the next throw, the next sprint, the next punt... his eyes fixed on the goal post at the far end of the field. Perhaps it was Rainey, the perpetual globe trotter, who inspired John to embark on a business venture to South America.

John's ambitions in the real estate market also landed him in a little trouble. The Paul J. Rainey Company was the defendant in a lawsuit filed by a man who ironically became John de Saulles's best friend. Marshall Eugene Ward would be one of the supper guests at John's home on the night of the fatal shooting, a pall bearer at the funeral, and a witness at the murder trial.

Marshall E. Ward came from humble beginnings in Louisville, Kentucky. His family was not famous. He did not attend an Ivy league college. He was never listed in the *Who's Who* or the social register. In 1905, he worked as a clerk in the Title Guarantee and Trust company in New York City. He lived in an apartment on West Eighth Street[24] in Greenwich Village with his older brother Horatio J. Ward, his mother Mary, and his stepfather

Newton W. Hartwell. The new head of the household, an inventor, aspired to follow on the heels of Thomas Edison and Alexander Graham Bell but never achieved his dreams. Like the character of Scarlett O'Hara in *Gone with the Wind*, the hardships of his impoverished youth gave Marshall a sense of desperation to never go hungry again, no matter what he had to do. He gravitated towards the charismatic John de Saulles and latched onto his coattails.

The legal dispute began in the fall of 1909 when the Paul J. Rainey Pier Company hired Marshall E. Ward to sell mortgage bonds for a commission of 10 percent on all bonds sold. He entered into a transaction with Miss Mary Reilly, a dressmaker who wanted to invest her life savings in mortgage bonds. She sent a check for $30,000 to Marshall at the Title Guarantee and Trust company, but later discovered that the company was only the trustee of the bonds and did not guarantee them. Miss Reilly sued the trust company and recovered her money, with interest, by proving in court that Marshall Ward had misrepresented the facts to her. The judge's written opinion on the Reilly lawsuit portrays Marshall and an out-and-out liar, who told her such things as the National Bank of Brooklyn had already subscribed to $125,000 worth of these bonds, and that his own sweet mother had invested

$25,000. In reality, neither the bank nor his mother had ever invested in the mortgage bonds.

The sales commission agreement with Paul J. Rainey Pier Co. also carried a sweetener whereby Marshall Ward and John de Saulles would separately pocket a 50 percent stock bonus, but this speculative amount was not part of Miss Reilly's complaint. Marshall Ward also filed a lawsuit because he was not paid his 10 percent commission for the sale of bonds to Miss Reilly, and John representing Paul J. Rainey Pier Co. answered that they owed him nothing because the sale never finalized. The lower court had judged in Marshall's favor and Paul J. Rainey Pier Co. filed an appeal. The matter dragged into March 1912 when the New York Supreme Court reversed the earlier judgment and ordered the lower courts to hold a new trial.[25] Yet despite their wrangling over sales commissions and lawsuits, the two became close friends.

In his personal life, as he padded his bank account and turned 30 years old, John de Saulles had not yet found true love among the dainty chiffon ladies of New York's high society. Women of the time were strange, doll-like creatures as described by contemporary novelist Edith Wharton, "in which it was the recognized custom to attract masculine homage while playfully discouraging it." He socialized with the opposite sex when the occasion demanded his presence but he preferred the sanctuary of fraternities and gentlemen's clubs. Among his fellow men, he could laugh out loud, enjoy a good cigar, and put his feet on the table. He bragged about his determination to avoid the ball-and-chain of matrimony as long as possible.

The vaudeville star Elsie Janis described meeting Jack "Kid" de Saulles around this time, when she was merely sixteen in her debutante season. Already a sensational child star with a savvy mother to manage her career, Elsie frolicked merrily in the New York City nightlife in between her stage appearances and on-the-road tours. In her autobiography *So Far! So Good!* she lists over a dozen of gentlemen on a single page, describing "…what wonderful times we had, and how fortunate for me, with my butterfly complex of that period… Every night, supper parties—Rector's was the favorite, the famous Metropole was next in my heart… Thanks, 'fellahs!' wherever you are, for the flowers, fruit, candy, books, food (no drinks in those days!), but most of all for starting me off right, with a correct valuation of the friendship of men!"[26]

Elsie Janis met "Kid" de Saulles again the following summer, when she was "nearly a year older and at least ten years more sensitive to masculine charms, of which the Kid had more than any one man merited! Ace Yale football player, sportsman, adventurer, fascinator of women. He had graduated in all courses of the school of experience, and I was not even qualified for kindergarten! ... You can imagine Mother's state of mind during this period of adolescent idiocy! My work in the theatre was just a "side-line"... Kid's gardenias meant more than the 'Standing Room Only' sign to me!"[27] Actually, her attentions were divided between three men who "had special privileges, such as driving me home from the theatre alone!—closely followed by Mother and the other members, taking me skating at St. Nicholas Rink, which was just across the street from the hotel, being asked to remain after the others had gone, and most important of all, rating entire pages in the Diary!"[28] Besides John de Saulles, she admired the gleaming smile of another Yale alumni Adolphus "Happy" Busch Magnus, the grandson of Adolphus (Anheuser) Busch the beer tycoon.

The candy and flowers came to an end when Elsie Janis embarked on a vacation to Europe in June 1906. She describes her family and her suitors gathering on the dock to wish her *bon voyage*. Despite her excitement at her first ocean voyage, when the ship started to move, she felt overwhelmed with regrets and second thoughts. Her tear-drenched eyes gazed back to shore at "Happy" and "the Kid" standing side-by-side to wave good-bye. "I preferred to think of them, rapiers in hand, fighting for my favor! What a ridiculous brat I was. They told me afterward that they went to Rector's and got tight together, while I walked the decks in utter misery..."[29] Eventually, she moved on to love other men such as the actor John Barrymore but would always be glad to receive occasional visits from "the Kid" in her theater dressing room. "He was never really absent… until years later when he passed out of life's picture so tragically."[30]

John's good ol' college buddies pranked him, twice, with fake engagement announcements sent to the newspapers. The first in 1907 rumored him engaged to Miss Elsie Moore[31] after they were both members of a bridal party at the wedding of her brother in Nashville. Again in 1910 his name was linked to a banker's daughter Miss Eleanor G. Brown soon after his business partner H.R. Talbot's wedding where John had served as best man and she was the maid of honor. In both cases, the fathers of the girls denied the reports. John was not amused the second time when a large pile of congratulations stuffed the mailbox at his Fifth Avenue office. He stomped over to the newspaper's headquarters to declare that when he found out the identity of the prankster, he hoped it was a man so he could pay him back with "a punch in the nose."[32] The prank was not repeated.

John de Saulles is listed in the 1911 edition of *Who's Who in New York City and State*, which gives his occupation as real estate, the president of the Paul J. Rainey Co., a member of the Phi Delta Phi fraternity and Yale's secret Book and Snake society. John's favorite recreational activity is reported as "shooting."

John Married Blanca

*I looked upon him as some young god
who had come from a strange and happy heaven
to make me happy.*

BLANCA ERRÁZURIZ VERGARA
(MRS. JOHN L. DE SAULLES)

Fate and a railroad enterprise sent John de Saulles to Santiago, Chile. He represented the South American Concessions Syndicate, made up largely of Americans living in London, to promote the Transandine Railroad (*Ferrocarril Trasandino*) connecting the railway systems of Chile and Argentina.[33] When eventually completed on April 16, 1910, after fifty years in development, the railways allowed a passenger to travel 800 miles from Buenos Aires to Valparaiso in a couple of days instead of taking an 11-day sea voyage around the continent's southernmost tip. Trains climbed to an impressive altitude above 10,000 feet and passed through a two-mile tunnel blasted through the Andes mountains. At the summit of the mountain pass, a statue was erected of Christ the Redeemer (*Christo Redemptor*) molded out of decommissioned cannons supplied by Argentina and Chile. The statue that still stands today is a token of the peaceful relationship between the two republics following the settlement of their boundary dispute that made the Transandine Tunnel possible. On the pedestal of the colossal statue is inscribed this dedication: "Sooner shall these mountains crumble into dust than the people of

Argentina and Chile break the peace which they have sworn to maintain at the feet of Christ the Redeemer."[34]

John traveled to Chile as the partner of Edward P. Coyne, a former New York judge, who provided legal counsel for an affiliate venture the British-Chilean Longitudinal Railroad Construction Company. The two had been friends since John's graduation from Yale Law School and John de Saulles had served as usher at Judge Coyne's wedding. The judge was a bit of a flamboyant character, a trial lawyer not afraid to take on controversial clients such as defending race track owners from restrictive legislation. A New York native, the son of immigrant Irish farmers, Coyne first married the daughter of a church minister and lived in the small town of Geneseo in western New York state. His second marriage broke up in 1909, after only a year, mainly due to the difference in their ages; the bride Mary Gatins was 22 and Judge Coyne was about 50 years old. When their marriage hit the rocks, Judge Coyne sailed away to London and Mary took off to Reno, Nevada to file the necessary papers. John de Saulles gave a quote to the *New York Times*, "It was plain to those who saw Judge Coyne before he sailed that he was a stricken man." Mr. Gatins, the girl's father, also shared an opinion with the papers. "Personally I have nothing against my daughter's husband. He is a fine gentleman. My objection to the marriage was not based on his personality, but on the difference between his age and that of my daughter. The result merely proves, as it has proved so often before, that a union between so old a man and so young a woman can mean nothing but misery and trouble for both."[35]

❦

John de Saulles met the lovely 16 year old Blanca Errázuriz on the sunny beach of Viña del Mar, in February or March 1911, the southern hemisphere's summer. She reclined in an easy chair beneath a shade tree among a group of the loveliest young senoritas in Chile trying *not* to get a tan. John attracted her attention by winning a friendly swimming race in the sparkling blue bay. When he emerged from the splashing surf, dripping wet and grinning, Blanca boldly asked to be introduced to the American.

He was 33 years old, but being handsome, athletic, and full of fun-loving spirit, he appeared younger. A slender and majestic woman, at 5 foot 7 inches[36] she was just one inch short of matching John's height. Even at this young age she did not seem youthful. Her early photographs have a Mona Lisa sort of grace, an ageless serenity that deepens her calm dark eyes. From that moment, he could not get her out of his thoughts.

He competed against her other suitors at the local country club, attempting the game of polo although he did not ride a horse very well. Football and baseball were played with his own two feet solidly on the ground. I imagine he galloped in circles and swung

41

his mallet wildly without scoring a point. Blanca giggled demurely at his fumbles. John, red-faced with embarrassment, flashed her a bright smile. He may have lost at the polo match but he felt like a winner.

John continued trying to woo her over the next few months, as the weather cooled heading into the southern hemisphere's autumn and winter. He did not have an easy path to the object of his affections with her mother and older sister always looming as chaperones. The rules of decorum and etiquette in Chile were as strict as polite society in New York, if not more so, and one has to wonder if he was almost ready to give up and call it a game.

Heart-breaking news reached John in August 1911 that his friend, Coley Carnegie, had died. While on a fishing trip in New York state's Adirondacks Mountains with his mother and sister, he contracted pneumonia and passed away before a doctor could come to his aid. Coley was only thirty-one years old, about two years younger than John. This tragedy kicked his adrenaline into high gear. No longer was the pretty Chilean heiress an exotic diversion in a foreign land. He decided to change his life by getting married, before it was too late, and he fixed his sights upon her.

When Blanca and her mother departed in October 1911 for a vacation in France, he hopped aboard a steamship and followed in their wake. There, in the city of love, he continued courting her.

Paris in the autumn transformed into a fairyland of rainbow pastels as gold and crimson leaves sprinkled to the blue cobblestone streets. Refreshing breezes off the Seine River cooled the brows of artists standing with easels, capturing the leisurely moment in pastels. The first nip of winter rustled the dry branches overhead. Flocks of white swans migrated south. They strolled, hand in hand, past dress shops and feathered hat shops and narrow bistros on lopsided avenues painted by Van Gogh and Renoir not so long ago. John bought her flowers and coaxed out of her porcelain-mask face one of her rare smiles.

At the first the family opposed the union because of the age and cultural differences, but John pushed forward to score his goal. He told the newspapers, "I just made up my mind that she was the loveliest girl in the world and I wanted her for my wife. It was no easy task either, for she had suitors galore. Until I went to Chile, all it meant to me was a long pink strip on a map in my geography. Now it means the world and all there is in it."[37]

Blanca quickly fell in love with the handsome, aggressive American and gave him unquestioning devotion. Water-blue eyes, a bright smile, and a shameless outgoing personality made him exotic and refreshing, the kind of man she had never known before. She said, "Americans are the finest men in the world. The Latins and the French may have better manners and more polish, but the Americans are big, generous, and trustworthy."[38] Years later, when interviewed in jail after killing John, she could still reminisce on these fond memories of their early days. "I looked upon him as some young god who had come from a strange and happy heaven to make me happy."[39]

The dazzled teenaged girl agreed to marry him while in Paris, and John insisted on rushing the wedding so that he could bring her back to the United States as his bride.[40] They had to get special permission from the Vatican because John had been baptized in the Episcopalian church. Although the wedding was arranged in a hurry, they still managed a beautiful lace gown and all the trimmings.

They married in Paris on December 14, 1911 at St. Joseph's church on the Avenue Hoche[41] built in 1869 to serve the small English-speaking ethnic community in Paris. John showed his rebellious and independent streak with this semi-elopement, a tendency to do things his own way. No one from his immediate family was given time to take a steamship across the Atlantic. Only his friend from New York, Judge Coyne, stood as best man.

The newly blessed Mr. and Mrs. John L. de Saulles honeymooned in France for a few weeks, taking time to visit John's grandmother at the family's villa in the south of France.

John's grandfather Louis de Saulles had been an ethnic French Huguenot of obscure origins who had immigrated by way of England to the state of Louisiana in the 1830s. This patriarch of the American branch of the family had traveled alone as a young, single man seeking his fortune in a new world. Those were the boom days in New Orleans when merchant ships crowded the seaport and steam driven riverboats chugged down the Mississippi River. Cotton, sugar, and tobacco made quick millionaires out of ordinary men. Louis de Saulles literally became a rags-to-riches success story, and with his exotic foreign accent and charming smile attracted the eye of Miss Armide Longer. She was one of several daughters in a prominent New Orleans family, her maiden name preserved as John Longer de Saulles's middle name. John honored his *grandmere's* heritage by his signature that always included the letter "L."

His grandfather Louis de Saulles had gained a fortune in exporting cotton, enough to maintain a summer home in Brookline, Massachusetts and to provide a luxurious antebellum lifestyle for his three sons and three daughters. Their historic mansion still stands at 2618 Coliseum Street in the Garden District of New Orleans, and the exterior façade with its Italianate architecture has changed very little since the house was first built in 1844. Its black shutters frame high narrow windows. Symmetrical columns support the second floor balcony and rows of tiny brackets at the eaves form a decorative edge like wooden cake frosting around the square, flat roof.

When the boom days of cotton and sugar started to show a decline in the years leading up to the Civil War, Louis de Saulles sold off the plantation in 1854 and never looked back. He relocated his family to New York City to be closer to where the eldest son Henry de Saulles studied at Harvard University in Cambridge, Massachusetts. The second son (John's father) Arthur de Saulles attended the Rensselaer Polytechnic Institute in New England, and immediately after graduation went on assignment to survey mining and metallurgical operations in northern Pennsylvania. Arthur then continued his higher education at the prestigious *École des Mines* college in Paris where he studied civil engineering.

John's grandparents had stayed in New York only a few years while the tensions between the northern and southern states escalated. Just before the Civil War broke out, Louis de Saulles returned to the Old World, bringing his family to the south of France and leaving behind the United States for the rest of his life. They settled into a villa in a picturesque town called Pau at the foothills of the Pyrenees Mountains near the border of Spain, a serene valley of emerald grass and wild flowers. Louis passed away in the mid-1880s, leaving behind his widow Armide Longer, several daughters who had married French men, and his sons who had returned to the United States.

John de Saulles enjoyed his honeymoon visit with his widowed grandmother, hearing the romantic stories of how she and his grandfather had met, and no doubt looking forward to the same sort of long and fruitful marriage for himself. Soon after Christmas

Day 1911, he said good-bye to his *grandmere* and, with his blushing young wife under his arm, boarded a steamship bound for New York.

๛

By crossing the ocean, Blanca abandoned her identity as a Chilean debutante with a Parisian soul. At the time of her marriage, Blanca automatically became a U.S. citizen. Until the law changed with the Married Woman's Act of 1922 (42 Stat. 1021), a foreign wife of an American man did not need to formally apply in court for citizenship. Thus, there are no immigration papers filed for Blanca; her wedding ring was enough.

"I will work to win the world and lay it at your feet,"[42] John said to Blanca as they leaned on the railing of the steamship *Baltic* pulling into New York's harbor on January 8, 1912. His strong arm clamped around her waist. She cuddled close to his side and shivered at the chilly sea breezes. Her dark eyes widened to behold the Statue of Liberty's silhouette against the city's rising skyline. Together they gazed at the endless sky as John recited grand promises of the wonderful life they would soon have.

Fig. 8 - John L. de Saulles, circa 1914

A few days after landing at Ellis Island and trying to keep a low profile, John and his lovely young bride were spotted at the auto show in New York's Madison Square Garden.[43] He had been away from the United States for over a year and could not resist checking out the newest models of automobiles. Some of the exciting, inventive gadgets and accessories being demonstrated were the ignition devices and electric headlights that operated from the dash by the turn of a switch! John's friends cornered him and pulled him away from the Everett Six-48 roadster. They threw him an impromptu wedding reception right there at one of the display booths. Beer—not champagne—toasted the happy beautiful couple posing on the running boards of boat-sized town cars.

Reporters intruded on the honeymooners at the Hotel Plaza and described Blanca de Saulles breezing in the door from a shopping trip on Fifth Avenue. "It was Mrs. de Saulles' first trip to New York, and she was disappointed. Oh no, not with New York. That she thought about the most wonderful place she had ever dreamed of, but New York's dancing—that's what she didn't like. 'Why I never saw such dancing as they do in New York,' said she. 'They hop and run and skip and wiggle—oh, it's perfectly absurd. I haven't danced once since I came here, and I had always looked forward to being able to come to New York to dance.'"[44]

Fig. 9 - Mrs. John L. de Saulles (circa 1912 - 1915)

Dancing and honeymooning passed all too soon. Blanca got pregnant within the first few months of marriage but probably did not realize it right away. She assumed her fatigue and queasiness came from too much dancing, too rich American food, and too much happiness.

They returned to Chile together for John to finish his business with the Transandine Railroad project. It was turning to summer in New York, but in Chile the cold, gray rainy days of winter had begun. Some work still had to be done finishing the Chilean end of the railroad line. As recounted in a letter to Archibald Johnston (vice-president of Bethlehem Steel Corporation) from John's colleague Mr. Dewey trying to reach Chile from Argentina in 1912: "We traveled for two hours over very difficult and dangerous bridle paths and then the snow was so deep we were obliged to walk. Sinking into the snow up to our hips very frequently, and in that altitude... it was very hard, and out of the question for any woman."

Snug and warm by the shores of Viña del Mar, I imagine that Blanca de Saulles made the joyous announcement to her mother, Doña Blanca, that she was going to produce the first grandchild of this generation. Mother and daughter started making plans to decorate one of the many spacious rooms in the Quinta Vergara palace as a nursery. Servants tended to her every need, and life settled into an effortless routine. Her spinster sister Amalia—who resembled her almost like a twin—cuddled and giggled at her side, making plans for when she would be an aunt.

Despite the gloomy weather raining on the lofty window panes, Blanca felt more blissful in these couple of months than she ever had before.

A letter from Archibald Johnston written to a colleague reports that, "Mr. de Saulles is here in all his glory and looks fine. He and his bride seem to be extremely happy." Secure on her home turf, with her husband whom she called Dada at her side, a dainty little bulge of tummy expanded the waistline of her stylish gowns. In April 1912, she celebrated her 18th birthday as a mother-to-be; in May of that year, John turned 34 years old.

Election 1912

*...college men have not borne a very active relationship
to public life in this country in the past.*

WOODROW WILSON
PRESIDENT OF THE UNITED STATES

In late July 1912, John received an offer to help with the Democratic National Committee's election campaign for Governor Woodrow Wilson to be the next president. The chairman William McCombs personally invited John to participate in the campaign efforts. John heard the coach's whistle blow and he sprang into action. He closed up his temporary office in Valparaiso and booked passage on the next steamship out of town. His pregnant wife—now in her fifth or sixth month—tagged along rather than be left behind.

Winter snows had buried the treacherous new railroad route through the Andes mountains, and so John did not have a chance to take advantage of the project he had helped to develop. They sailed the long way around Cape Horn and lost about two weeks. Always thinking fast on his feet, John made a strategy to shortcut the curve of the Earth by transferring steamships via Europe. They arrived at New York's Ellis Island for the second time that year, on August 5, 1912, aboard the steamship *Amerika*.

Despite of the rigors of his journey around half the globe, John hit the ground running. "We are already in the field with our uniforms on," he said, "and are lined up for a Wilson touchdown. Our flying wedge will sweep the country from Maine to California."[45] John stayed in New York busy organizing the Woodrow Wilson College Men's League with headquarters at the Hotel Imperial on 32nd Street and Broadway. He served as treasurer which included the duties of fundraiser and publicist.

They took a temporary residence in the community of Larchmont, New York, on the northern shore of Long Island Sound. This area was becoming an exclusive get-away for the upper crust of society. Resort hotels and summer cottages provided a sanctuary for vacationers looking to play golf at the country club or take romantic buggy rides under the autumn leaves. This is where the silent film stars Douglas Fairbanks and Mary Pickford would first meet and fall in love.

Soon after their arrival, when her pregnancy started to show, John sent Blanca to stay at his parents' home in Bethlehem, Pennsylvania. He was too busy with the election campaign to care for her properly and assumed that she would be in good hands with his mother. He made occasional visits there, on the weekends, but for the most part Blanca was alone through the final stages of her pregnancy. It was the first separation of their brief marriage.

The hard-working industrial town in the shadow of Bethlehem Steel corporation was a dismal contrast to the sunny beach of Viña del Mar or the excitement of cities like Paris, London, or New York. The de Saulles's three-story, shingled manor house on Delaware Avenue in the Fountain Hill neighborhood was the best that Bethlehem had to offer, but its gabled windows and red brick chimney shrank in comparison to the Palacio Vergara. The weather turned gray and rainy, plunging Blanca into a winter-time depression by re-living the dark seasons of the southern hemisphere all over again in the United States.

Some Background on John's Parents

John's father Arthur de Saulles was a Civil War veteran who had fought for the Confederacy and proudly went by the term "Major" for the rest of his life. He had served not as cannon fodder but on the staff of the civil engineer corps under Major Lovell. Rapidly advancing to the rank of major himself, Arthur had managed such projects as constructing fortifications of earthworks near Lake Pontchartrain and building pontoon trains to transport military supplies to the front line.

When the war ended in 1865, Arthur de Saulles did not stay in the defeated South but traveled abroad to Europe to finish college. After completing his bachelor's degree, he returned to the U.S. to work as a civil engineer for the New York & Schuylkill Coal Company near Wilkes-Barre, Pennsylvania.

Arthur de Saulles married John's mother Catharine M. Heckscher on August 19, 1869[46], a few months before his 30th birthday. Theirs was a mixed marriage of Southern and Yankee, as well as French and German heritage, but they stayed together almost 50 years until Arthur's death. She was born in New York City on December 5, 1840, a member of a prominent family of bankers who had emigrated recently from Hamburg, Germany[47]. Her father Charles A. Heckscher came to New York in the 1830s and thrived as a merchant dealing mainly with the coal industry. In their first year of marriage, Arthur and Catherine de Saulles lived a simple life in the township of South Cass near the tiny coal mining village of Heckscherville (owned by Catherine's family) in Schuylkill County, Pennsylvania.[48] He attended the first meeting of the American Institute of Mining, Metallurgical, and Petroleum Engineers in May 1871 and is credited with being one of AIME's founding members.

Arthur and Catherine moved to New Jersey after the company that he worked for sold out to the Philadelphia and Reading Coal & Iron Company.[49] He stayed for about five years and started a family in Orange, New Jersey, the town later made famous when Thomas Edison established his research laboratory and factories there.

Dunbar Furnace Company hired Arthur de Saulles as vice-president and superintendent, and the family relocated farther inland to the coal mining region of Lehigh Valley in eastern

Pennsylvania. Around the time that John and his younger sister Caroline were born, Arthur de Saulles came to be the superintendent of the New Jersey Zinc Company's operations in South Bethlehem—a company formerly owned by Catherine's cousin August Heckscher.

Arthur de Saulles kept a low profile as a quiet, sincere man generally liked by his peers. In politics he was "a good old fashioned democrat."[50] As superintendent of the factory, he was not a tycoon at heart and never desired to be the next Andrew Carnegie or Charles M. Schwab. He teamed up with George Converse in 1902 to patent a couple of inventions for the processing of zinc and zinc by-products.[51] The "Converse–de Saulles Furnace" set a standard to be referenced in engineering journals for years to come. He worked for the New Jersey Zinc Company until his retirement in 1911. Even then, he continued his involvement in metallurgy and the smelting of zinc in collaboration with his son Charles who later followed in his footsteps as an engineer.

At the time of his death in December 1917, Arthur de Saulles was a vestryman of the local Episcopalian Church of the Nativity and president of the Men's Club at the church. His biography in the AIME Journal ends with this heartfelt epitaph, "His kindly nature led him to take an active interest in the promotion of healthful sports among young men. He was ever active in all things pertaining to the general welfare and uplift of his fellowmen. In his death the profession has lost a distinguished engineer and metallurgist and our country a patriotic able citizen and man of affairs—one greatly beloved by those whom he honored with his friendship, and respected and looked up to by all who were privileged to know him."[52]

Blanca would later complain that the in-laws were harsh and unfriendly to her, but Mr. and Mrs. de Saulles maintained they were nothing but kind. In all honesty, I imagine they were cliquish but for John's sake made a superficial effort to be gracious. Although they were too polite to say it to her face, they could not help being racist. They knew nothing of Chile or her illustrious ancestors, and their minds compared Blanca to the local Hispanic and Italian immigrants digging canals, laying bricks, and building bridges. On the other hand, the last trimester of pregnancy is the worst time in anyone's life to make acquaintance of a new husband's family. Blanca had to speak English at all times, and although fluent, being immersed in a second language is always a strain. She missed her mother and her own home. Painful memories resurfaced from the years that she spent in boarding school, separated from her family, surrounded by blue-eyed foreigners, a fish out of water gasping for breath.

While his young pregnant wife was in the care of his parents, John de Saulles blossomed in the arena of political activism. The Wilson College Men's League was unique at the time for activating an untapped resource. Woodrow Wilson made a speech on September 28, 1912 at a dinner hosted by the League, and said, "It must be admitted, to our shame, that college men have not borne a very active relationship to public life in this country in the past."[53] Other demographic groups were starting to organize labor unions in the factories and mills, but until this point, the students at colleges were a haven of intellectual neutrality. Wilson himself had been the president of Princeton University and was thrust into a political office that he did not actively pursue. He called upon his fellow collegians to tread in his footsteps. Because of Woodrow Wilson, college students started to become politically active.

The presidential election of 1912 parallels the Obama campaign of 2008 as a time when the American people desired a change from the status quo. The Republican party had been in power for a number of years and the incumbent president William Howard Taft had sinking popularity. A few episodes of financial slumps had everyone worried about the future economy. Teddy Roosevelt, the former president from years back, returned from retirement to try and regain his seat in the White House. In a role similar to Senator John McCain in 2008 who contrasted to the youthful Barack Obama, "Roosevelt was the battle scarred veteran whose rallying call had thrilled a generation. Wilson was a bright figure burst suddenly onto the stage, lucid, rational, calling men to a higher vision of themselves and their destiny."[54] As a former Princeton man, Wilson was strongly supported by the academic community who perceived him as the intellectual candidate who could give thoughtful analysis to the new problems facing the country in the twentieth century.

The College Men's League committee had a formal structure of William B. Hornblower as president, and Joseph R. Truesdale as secretary, but John L. de Saulles as treasurer became the face for the movement. He was the man with the Peter Pan smile who could not believe (or would not admit) that he was actually 34 years old and still behaved like he just graduated college yesterday. He reached out to the youth and they responded. Like the Obama campaign when students quickly set up campaign offices with laptops and cell phones, the college men in 1912 used the latest technology available. They called each other on the telephone and sent telegrams. They gathered at campuses, fraternity houses, and community centers. They traveled by automobile to spread the word.

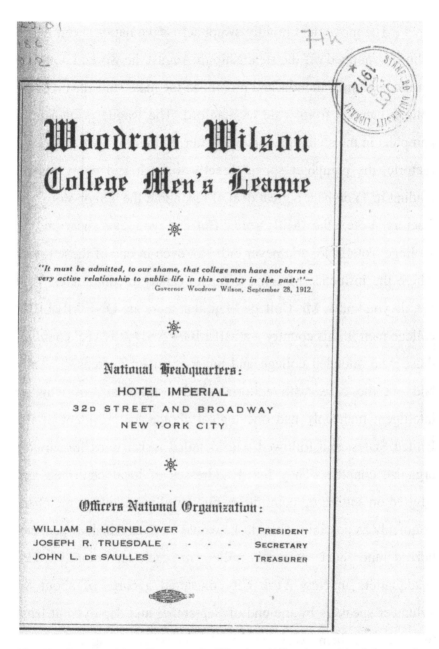

Fig. 10 - the appeal to college men for Woodrow Wilson's presidential campaign

61

The movement rapidly swept across the nation. From when John first hopped off the steamship in August, he worked non-stop for the next three months and mobilized the male students on every college campus from Yale to Stanford. The league printed up a pamphlet in the style of a personal letter. Rather than dry campaign rhetoric, the pamphlet spoke directly to each and every person reading it. "You hear a great deal of talk about the 'Labor Vote,' the 'Factory Vote,' the 'Mill Vote.' But did you ever hear of the 'College Vote'? No, you never did. Not even in one of those towns where the influence of some great university predominates. And yet, do you know, Mr. College Man, that there are ONE MILLION college men in this country—a MILLION AND A HALF counting those who attended college and never received degrees?"[55] They laid out the case, with editorials and testimonials, of why an intelligent man only had one logical choice for president of the United States, and followed with detailed instructions for how to organize chapters. They listed addresses of local chairmen and advised on setting up committees and enrolling as many members as quickly as possible. Their tasks would be to establish a speaker's bureau and host political rallies in each community. The headquarters in New York City mustered a corps of about 80 volunteer speakers by the end of September and deployed at least two dozen of them every evening. College men arranged for town hall meetings, spoke eloquently about Wilson to their friends and neighbors, and volunteered to watch the polls on election day.

The brilliance of this grass roots approach expanded Wilson's campaign beyond his immediate circle of cronies and used the untapped limitless resources of volunteerism. Before the days of television and radio, they could not quickly reach out to millions of people by printing up campaign flyers and mailing them out. One short booklet to each university in the country activated thousands of eager college students who spread the message exponentially. The College Men's League pamphlet advised, "A personal letter to a college friend is worth more than a dozen booklets."[56] Teddy Roosevelt making personal appearances on a whistle-stop tour simply could not keep up with them.

In this same pamphlet, John de Saulles wrote an appeal for campaign contributions. Although Teddy Roosevelt had split with the Republican party and promoted himself as a progressive, creating his own "Bull Moose" party, he would be criticized by Wilson's campaign for accepting contributions from large corporations. Wilson advertised himself as a genuine progressive Democrat supported by regular folks—a man of the people—and actually turned away campaign contributions from donors in big business. The country was hungry for change; the question was which path to choose.

REQUEST FOR CONTRIBUTIONS

The National Woodrow Wilson College Men's League has been organized for the purpose of enlisting aid in the election of Woodrow Wilson.

It is essential to raise funds to carry on the work of this college league, and to the college men who desire the election of Woodrow Wilson, we are making an apeal for financial assistance.

Should you care to contribute, a receipt for your contribution will be sent you in the form of a lithographed certificate.

It will certify that the holder has contributed to the National Campaign. The denominations of these certificates are $1, $2, $5, $10, $25, $100, $500 and $1,000. All remittances should be made to John L. de Saulles, Treasurer, Hotel Imperial, Thirty-second Street and Broadway, New York City, or to the Treasurer of your State Organization.

Even without a monetary contribution we would ask you to send to Headquarters any suggestions you may care to make which, in your mind, would aid in the success of this National college movement for Woodrow Wilson.

Believe me,

Very sincerely yours,

(Signed) JOHN L. DE SAULLES,
National Treasurer.

Fig. 11 - John's request for contributions to the college men's league

Women suffragists were lobbying at this time for the right to vote, an issue on which Wilson was ambiguous and non-committal. They hoped that by contributing their efforts in the campaign, they could put pressure on Wilson to recognize women as a political asset. Ironically, Wilson did not have a son; he had three adult daughters who were unable to cast their votes for their own father. While promoting himself as a progressive Democrat, the man who would change the old political machinery in Washington D.C. and reform the age-old corrupt practices of a Republican administration, Wilson's personal beliefs placed him on the conservative side of women's suffrage. This is another parallel to Barack Obama who appealed to the progressive elements in the Democratic Party during the campaign but disappointed his liberal supporters after the election. President Wilson's feet would also be held to the fire. The 19th Amendment granting women the right to vote would not become reality for another eight years at the very end of Wilson's second term.

As Election Day 1912 drew near, John de Saulles felt confident of victory. John and the College Men's League vice-president Joseph Truesdale were inspired to throw a parade in New York for the Saturday before the election. They coordinated around Woodrow Wilson's busy schedule of last-minute public speeches and rousing the faithful to get out the vote on the coming Tuesday. John de Saulles told the *New York Times*, "The demonstration will amount to a good old-fashioned spontaneous Democratic rally, where marchers can voluntarily fall into line and make an enormous escort, making Broadway, with its blaze of lights, a sight worth going miles to see... Never has such a thing been done, and it will be, so the college men say, a fitting tribute to their work for the last several weeks."[57]

As treasurer of the league, John sent last-minute letters and telegrams to the branch offices asking for funds. The *Times-Dispatch* printed one of John's letters on November 1, 1912 as received by the Virginia College Men's League's state chairman.

"What promises to be the biggest parade and demonstration in political history is to be held in New York November 2. Members of this league are to lead the line of march, with Woodrow Wilson at the head. The parade is being given under the auspices of the Woodrow Wilson College Men's League, which is standing for all expenses, including bands, grandstands, flags, banners, floats, advertising, etc. The cost of the same will be in the neighborhood of $20,000. All political and patriotic societies supporting Woodrow Wilson are turning out en masse. One hundred thousand men are expected to fall in line. It is our purpose to make this contribution to the national committee in the name of the league. It would be a fitting close to the splendid work carried on by this league throughout the country. As treasurer of the organization I need all the assistance and help that I can possible get in order to carry out our ambition, and I am calling on the members of the Virginia League to give me financial support. Do not feel that Saturday will be the end, because the bills will come in next week, and that is the time that I need the money the most. Whatever your organization can do will be more than appreciated. Please wire me if we can count on you for this much needed assistance."

The incumbent Vice-President of the United States, James Sherman, unexpectedly fell ill and died on October 30, 1912. Flags went to half-mast and the nation took a moment of silence in the midst of a bitter election campaign. The Wilson parade rally was rescheduled by a few days to show respect, but as they say on Broadway, the show must go on.

Rescheduling meant the busy candidate Woodrow Wilson was no longer available to ride at the head of the College Men's League parade. He had a fixed itinerary, so his daughter Margaret Wilson represented her father at the Hotel Imperial grandstand. This day was a foreshadowing of years to come, when Wilson's first wife Ellen would die of kidney disease and Margaret would stand in as temporary First Lady of the White House.

Coverage of the parade is described in great, colorful detail by the *New York Times* issue that hit the newsstands on Election Day November 5, 1912. Miss Wilson sat in a grandstand in front of the Hotel Imperial, joined by National Democratic Chairman William McCombs and several other members of the national campaign committee. The *New York Times* estimated about 60,000 people marched on Fifth Avenue and took almost an hour to pass the grandstand, where Miss Wilson bowed and smiled and waved a little American flag at the ranks beneath her. The parade got underway, by torchlight, around 8:00 PM with brass bands blaring from every street corner. A spotlight shined from the TIMES tower.

"Big Bill" Edwards, the commissioner of the city, served as Grand Marshal of the parade with aids at his side Joseph R. Truesdale and John L. de Saulles.

The commissioner's tallest stableman, at 7 feet 3 inches tall, dressed in a costume of Uncle Sam to lead the parade. Little children in a donkey cart followed behind Uncle Sam, carrying a sign: "Our daddies are going to vote for Wilson and Sulzer. We are the Young Democracy." College men marched under the banners of Princeton (Woodrow Wilson's alma mater), Yale, Harvard, Brown, Columbia, and many more. The collegians carried somewhat verbose printed slogans such as, "Woodrow Wilson - Herald of the Dawn of the Era of Good Feeling," and "The Way to Improve Your Mind is to Deliver the Goods." One slogan stands out as a little catchier and to the point: "For Better Team Work in the Real Game."

An actual, live 3,000 pound elephant borrowed from Luna Park played the part of the Republican Party with a sign pasted on her sides: "G.O.P. Legalized Monopoly of Broken Promises." Judy the elephant's wrangler, Paul Schwartz, told the reporters, "We gave her 100 pounds of hay and told her we'd take her to Manhattan to walk for Wilson... and she shook her head in great glee... She is for Wilson, just like everybody else from Coney Island."

About twenty floats (borrowed from Coney Island's Mardi Gras collection) portrayed caricatures of Teddy Roosevelt, President Taft, Andrew Carnegie, J.P. Morgan, and others. Performers dressed as the Gold Trust Twins kept busy with dishpans and scuttles loaded with imaginary corporation funds, a not-so-subtle allusion to the Republican Party's allegiance to big business. Papers fluttered out of an upper window from the Hotel Imperial, directly over Miss Wilson's head. She caught one of the yellow sheets that turned out to be a pamphlet of Roosevelt campaign songs. The lampooning of Teddy Roosevelt continued with a full-grown bull moose mounted on a wagon and two Standard Oil cans tied to its tail.

This is what John de Saulles knew best: team mascots, banners and pennants, slogans, pranks, and how to arouse the cheering fans. He understood intuitively how to exploit the mass media to promote a candidate and how to lampoon the opponent. Parades for a national election were supposed to be dignified affairs with brass bands marching in neat military lines. No one had ever behaved like this before. Candidates had never marketed themselves like a commodity. Political cartoons published in the newspapers mocked the candidates or the issues, but the campaigners themselves relied on the eloquence of their speeches and pamphlets or, in the case of Teddy Roosevelt, their personal charisma. Now we were entering the 20th century. The issues took a back seat to the glorious pageantry of it all. This campaign was the most photographed up to date, when cameras used silver nitrate film that captured action shots of Woodrow Wilson with his mouth open shouting out a speech from the caboose of a steam train. Not only newspaper reporters took pictures but crowds also took personal Kodak snapshots by the hundreds. Audio of Wilson's inauguration speech was captured on Thomas Edison's newly invented phonograph.

Woodrow Wilson was elected president on Tuesday, November 5, 1912 in a landslide vote. He obliterated his competition, carrying 40 states and 435 electoral votes compared to Teddy Roosevelt's 6 states and 88 electoral votes. The incumbent president Taft had only two states on his side. The fourth and most radical candidate, Debs, did little more than steal a few thousand votes from the others. Democrats took control of the White House and the Senate for the first time in 20 years.[58] Wilson accepted the news of his victory with an air of aloof detachment. Everyone around him clapped and cheered, but he remained cool. Telegrams of congratulations poured into his headquarters but he set most of them aside to read later. He retreated quietly into the company of his loving wife and three daughters. The real work had yet to begin.

Blanca de Saulles did not get to act like a trophy wife decorating her husband's sleeve at the national parade or celebrate the victory on Election Day. She was pregnant and snowbound at her mother-in-law's brick home in Pennsylvania. In those days women did not flaunt being "in the family way." They had no such thing as maternity clothes. No more corsets and stylish clothes and feathery big-brim hats. No more dancing. She felt heavy and matronly, and everything ached. She could not sleep because the restless little boy—she knew in her heart it was a boy—kicked her insides in the middle of the night.

Blanca was initiated into the Thanksgiving Day holiday about one month ahead of her delivery. I imagine that she experienced the cornucopia of a North American banquet table, a gigantic roast turkey with potato salad and all the trimmings, along with cakes and cookies from Mrs. de Saulles's German heritage. Perhaps she was introduced to her in-laws, John's three surviving siblings. The oldest brother Charles de Saulles had two little sons aged six and four, squirming in their seats. The older sister Armide McClintock had a teenaged daughter roughly the same age as Blanca, and the younger sister Caroline Degener had a school-aged daughter with flowing locks tied into a large satin bow.

Their son was born on Christmas Day 1912 in Bethlehem, Pennsylvania. In those days, typically babies were born at home; to use a hospital was a cultural shift that would happen decades later.

71

I assume Blanca de Saulles gave birth in her upstairs bedroom with a country doctor making a house call and a nurse at her side. I don't know if Blanca had an easy delivery or if she was traumatized by an experience for which she was so ill-prepared. I don't know if John traveled out from New York to be there, pacing nervously by the candle-lit *tanenbaum* in the living room while servants boiled water. I don't know what he felt—ecstatic or terrified—when holding the swaddled bundle like a fragile football in his arms. This critical moment changed them both from children into adults, from lovers into parents.

Fig. 12 - Blanca de Saulles and her son (1913)

Their son John Gerard Longer de Saulles Jr. was baptized on January 6, 1913[59] at the local Holy Infancy Roman Catholic church. The baby's godfather was the most prominent man in town: Charles M. Schwab the charismatic president of Bethlehem Steel Corporation. The event was staged like the crowning of a prince.

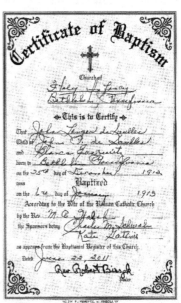

Fig. 13 - Baptism Certificate of John L. de Saulles, Jr. showing Charles M. Schwab as godfather

The landmark Gothic style church, constructed in 1883 at the corner of Fourth and Taylor streets, towered over everything else in the area. The exterior façade is of cream-colored sandstone imported from New Jersey. Today, after a century of weathering, its stones have darkened to gray. At the time of John de Saulles Jr.'s baptism, the building shined like gold.

I imagine Blanca carrying her swaddled bundle of joy, entering through lofty doors in a central tower with a spire. The color of Heaven's gates shined through the narrow stained glass windows. Brilliant reds, blues, purples, and greens cast a dappled pattern on the warm soft tones within. The interior walls of butter yellow glimmered with stencils of gold leaf, and the walnut pews polished to a high gloss appeared to be yellow jade. Over the splendid altar of white marble hung three panels of Renaissance style oil paintings depicting in life-sized glorious color the baby Jesus in his cradle, the Virgin Mary being carried up to Heaven on the wings of cherubs, and women weeping underneath the crucifixion of Jesus Christ.

Blanca's hometown church in Viña del Mar resembles the Holy Infancy church in the same neo-Gothic style architecture. *Nuestra Senora de los Dolores* also has a rectangular structure with narrow stained glass windows, a steeple rising over the front entrance, a rosette window over the door, a bell tower, a conical peak, and a cross high at the top. Of all the family gathered over the baptismal font in Bethlehem, only John knew what Blanca's parish church looked like. Only he could have guessed, because he had been there, what sentimental thoughts might have been going through her mind. The Pennsylvania church had stained glass windows, too, but it did not have the personal significance of saintly portraits that alluded to her ancestors. The priest spoke ancient Latin as he dribbled water over little Jack's wispy black hair and anointed his forehead with sacred oil, in the same ritual that a priest in Chile would have performed. If she closed her eyes, she could imagine the church bells ringing in this steeple were the bells of her home town.

After the baptism, John soon returned to New York City to earn a living in the real estate market. His days were filled with cocktail lunches at classy hotels and his nights were spent at the typewriter and the telegraph office. He lived in a man's world of barber shops and gentlemen-only clubs. The nightspots he haunted to entertain his high-powered clients were no place for a lady, especially one with a babe in arms.

Blanca stayed behind in Pennsylvania with her infant son. Separated for long periods from her busy husband, suffering from culture shock and post-partum depression, Blanca started on a downward spiral.

La Madre Dolorosa

Oh, Toodles, Daddy doesn't love us anymore!

BLANCA DE SAULLES

John attended President Wilson's inauguration ceremony in Washington D.C. on March 4, 1913, but Blanca was unable to be with him. A young mother with a newborn baby simply did not travel in the snow. He lived a vagabond life, going back and forth from his father's home in Pennsylvania to bachelor's rooms in New York's finest hotels and gentlemen's clubs.

John corresponded with Colonel Edward Mandell House, a close confidante of President Wilson, throughout the first year of the new administration. On May 7, 1913, from the Yale Club, he wrote, "Once again I must thank you for the kindly interest you have shown in my behalf. I can always be reached through my father's house at South Bethlehem, Penn. I take this opportunity of bringing to your attention the name of Archibald S. White of Ohio. Mr. White is also a candidate for a diplomatic post and has been very strongly recommended by our friend McCombs. It was when the latter was sorely in need of financial assistance in the late campaign that I personally brought Mr. White to Bill & Mr. White in turn responded most generously. Gov. Cox is particularly desirous of Mr. White's success & I believe he is even going to Washington for the sole purpose of furthering Mr. White's candidacy. Appreciating your friendly feeling towards McCombs

77

& his friends, I am taking this liberty of mentioning to you one who was so loyal to the cause & one who is so worthy of recognition. Believe me, with renewed thanks— Most sincerely— John L. de Saulles."

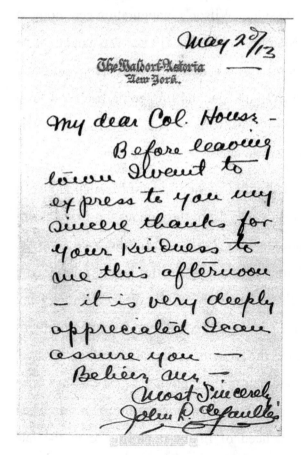

Fig. 14 - John L. de Saulles's personal letter to Col. Edward Mandell House

On January 29, 1914, John wrote from The Brook (one of the most exclusive gentleman's club in Manhattan), "My dear

Colonel House, Before you go south I want to thank you once again for the interest you have shown in my behalf and tell you that I deeply appreciate your sympathetic and invaluable aid. Wishing you a most enjoyable journey. Believe me— Most sincerely— John L. de Saulles."

The letters are fascinating not so much for their content but for the clues they give about John's life at that time. He did not have a permanent home or office address in New York city. Some letters are typewritten and show the scratches of a correction eraser. Some are in John's handwriting: a large, swift, hasty pen, at one point running low on ink but he pushed forward to finish the sentence in a fade-out. Before signing off "very sincerely yours," he closes every letter with the very formal expression, "Believe me..." which was commonly used in the 18th century but nearly obsolete by his lifetime. On the football field, he is a risk taker, but in his letter writing style he is reserved and traditional. He behaves like a young man, but he writes like his father.

Living apart from her husband, Blanca yearned for the exciting social life of a big city. Still youthful, not yet twenty years old, she missed dancing the Waltz under glittering chandeliers. No one at that time had ever heard of the idea of post-partum depression. She struggled with an infant through sleepless nights and chaotic days. While she dealt with the diapers and the bawling baby, albeit with the help of nursemaids and house servants.

Pennsylvania's heavy winter snows followed by a muggy summer did not improve her mood. She was a young girl alone with her first baby and living among strangers.

In the absence of her own mother, and unable to warm up to her Germanic mother-in-law, Blanca bonded emotionally with the nursemaid Ethel Whitesides. Before long, Ethel left employment to become Mrs. John O'Neill but Blanca continued to reach out to Ethel as a friend.

In one letter, dated June 17, 1913[60], Blanca wrote to Ethel O'Neill in the fictional voice of her six-month old son.

> *""Dear Nursie: I was so glad to get your nice letter this morning. Mother told me she had also heard from you, and we are all very glad to see that you have not forgotten us. The weather has been quite delightful up to the last three days, and these have been bad enough to cancel the pleasantness of the formers ones. I am sorry your 'new baby' has given you so much trouble, but you see, not all babies are such good little boys as I am. I am getting a tooth right in the middle of the upper gum, and I was so glad that no one had noticed it, because I wanted to give them all a surprise, but yesterday, playing 'patty cakes' with mother, I laughed and she saw it, and shrieked with glee. It isn't quite out yet, but you can see the little bump and it feels quite sharp. Mother wanted to keep it to herself, but Bessie found out, too. Mother has told her not to say a word so that when grandfather comes back, I shall laugh, and he will see it and give me a new dress.*

"Grandpa has been away since Friday in Atlantic City; father was away all last week and came back on Sunday, and left again Monday morning, and won't be back till next Friday. I am sending you a little package, which I hope you will like. I don't mean the package itself, but what's inside.

"I surprise the whole family now, but I'll surprise them more still. I can roll on my back when I'm lying on my tummy, and on to my tummy when I'm on my back. I've sat up of my own accord three times, and now I can put my toes in my mouth whenever I feel like it. Mother is looking for some cool place without mosquitoes, as she has been feeling quite sick in this heat, and as soon as she finds one we'll move. I miss you fearfully, but Bessie says that now I am her boy. She is very fond of me and thinks me wonderful. She is quite nice, and I suppose, by and by, when we know each other better, things will run as smoothly as before. She is very willing and does things as mother tells her. I hope we shall see you again before long.

With much love, ever your little TOODLES."

They did not return to Chile, as she hoped, but stayed in Pennsylvania for another whole year. After the birth of their son, it seems that John lost interest in his young wife, or so she later claimed. John spent more and more time away from home, pursuing his business ventures or socializing with his political network.

At Blanca's murder trial, the defense attorney's opening statement dramatized her unhappiness during this period of living

81

in the factory town. John would call on the telephone to announce his coming but fail to appear, or Blanca "frequently waited for him at the railroad station and was disappointed after his promises to come."[61] Her nursemaid Ethel O'Neill testified at trial of how John often stood her up. She described a time when Blanca collapsed to her knees at the cradle to weep over the baby, "Oh, Toodles, Daddy doesn't love us anymore!"

On the other hand, John's sister Caroline testified at the murder trial that Blanca stopped being a wife to him in every sense of the word. She became depressed, moody, and withdrawn. The way the de Saulles family told it, Blanca rejected him, not the other way around. Yet there was no obvious foreshadowing of Blanca being capable of violence. The stage actress Elsie Janis encountered the couple in the summer of 1913 at Narragansett Pier, Rhode Island and briefly commented in her memoirs, "You wouldn't have dreamed she could kill a man, least of all The Kid!"[62]

Blanca wrote a deluge of letters to John while he was away on business. Her letters were sentimental, child-like, sometimes silly, and show her painful mix of desperate loneliness and devotion to her absent husband. The selection of letters is limited, many of them lost (or destroyed) over the years. They are preserved only in transcripts of her divorce hearing and later used as evidence at her murder trial.

One letter dated June 22, 1913[63] reads as follows:

"Darling, Precious Dada: I feel so sad tonight, as I had been looking forward with so much eagerness to your coming. It is ages since you left, and I am wondering whether you have forgotten your little wife who awaits you anxiously, and your darling baby boy. I had ordered the runabout for this evening, thinking we would have a delightfully quiet and old fashioned drive during which we could tell each other all the many things we have to say. But, however much I was longing to see you, it is much better that you save yourself this unpleasant trip which in the end would only allow us a couple of hours together.

"I do hope you are well—I am so afraid that you don't take the proper amount of rest. You must not worry about Toodles or me. We are both doing remarkably well. He has taken to the bottle like a duck to water, and I am not having any trouble as we had anticipated. If we are having a hard pull, we have still a great many things to be thankful for. It is really wonderful how well Toodles is doing and how little cause for anxiety he has given us. It is a great thing that he has withstood the change of food so remarkably well. He liked even the first bottle I gave him—did not even mind my giving it to him, knowing as he does that I have him din-din; I, thank God, have not felt any pain nor feeling of uncomfort.

"So Dada, I am very happy that everything has gone so well and may it continue so. The weather has been quite delightful. Your mother and I are alone, your father having gone to Atlantic City, in order to take Nellie to Louise, to look after her children, since she had nobody to do so. I enclose the three

83

trolley car tickets which have been knocking about;
you may have occasion to use them, in case you
have no change in your pockets, besides saving 15
cents. 'Count the pence, and the pounds will take
care of themselves,' Fraulein used to say. Don't
disappoint me again, darling, and please come
Tuesday without fail. It's so lonesome without you,
and quite discouraging at times."

An undated letter[64], addressed to "Darling Dadda Boy," mentions her brother Guillermo ("Billy") Errázuriz marrying Maria Edwards MacClure. "I was so glad to get your note this morning and as I read today's omen, I hope it would be true. Many, many thanks for thinking of me and sending me that lovely cook book. As soon as we are in our little home we'll try them all, won't we? And we'll have such fun! Oh, what happiness it will be. Do call me up as soon as you know something definite, darling. I'm so excited and so anxious, I can hardly breathe. I have prayed all day for you and am sure God can't refuse. Hope you get my wire. Just think Billy got married already. I'm so very sad we weren't there for the wedding. The cable was addressed to us both."

Another letter written during the summertime[65] says, "I missed you very much. I feel so lonely now I don't know what to do. Could you find out from some one of some nice, cool place, with no mosquitoes, and nice drives where I could take you in a buggy? Darling, I don't wish to complain, because you are already having a hard time, but, precious, I'm afraid this heat will really make me sick, and dada, dear, I'm doing my best."

This letter dated July 25, 1913, written after an argument, is a bizarre mixture of sarcasm and passive anger.[66]

> *"Darling Dar, I have had a great big heartache ever since you told me to 'go to your room,' and I have made up my mind that I would not write to you until you wrote to me, or else spoke one sweet word through the phone, but I have relented, and instead am going to tell you how harsh and unkind you were. I did not think that ever in your lifetime if you were to live for a hundred years, would you have ordered me out of the room, much less gone away without saying good-bye or where you were going to stay. That—after a thousand and one professions of love! Well, I suppose every one's ideals are shattered, and yours probably also, although I have tried not to shatter yours, even when things did seem so hard. I hope you are having a good time in New York, it must be such fun to play bachelor again; in fact, it must seem quite natural, and the last two years surely are but a horrible nightmare— then so inopportunely the wife's letter comes. Why don't you race with Maurice and enjoy yourself? You will only get nervous and bored in Bethlehem and lose your appetite."*

John still had the restless energy of adventure in his soul and resisted being chained to a desk in a political role. He networked with politicians and public figures such as New York's recently elected mayor John P. Mitchel. He made friends with Mr. Dudley Field Malone the Collector of the Port (customs officer) at New York's harbor. John attended a public ceremony just before Thanksgiving 1913 when Malone took the oath of office.[67] But John did not actively pursue a public office for himself. There was talk in the newspapers of giving John a post in the White House cabinet but those plans never materialized. He was a father now, which can terrify even the best of men, and in his mid-30s had started to take a long hard look at what his life had been and what he yet wanted to accomplish.

Blanca's growing frustration and bitterness of the time are best illustrated in a letter she wrote in August 1913 to Ethel O'Neill.[68] Bear in mind she is 19 years old, her infant son is cutting his first teeth, and she is at odds with her mother-in-law.

> *"Mrs. de Saulles has almost got me frantic. I have to use the utmost strength of mind not to pull her hair; really I've been so patient and put up with so much that now my patience has turned into hate. Isn't that perfectly frightful? She is worse and worse from day to day. Now she wants to know why I don't go away, and keeps on asking me how much longer I'm going to stay—as if it were a pleasure for me to stay in a place which is exactly opposite in every way to the home I was brought up in. She ought to be thankful that her son has married a woman who has stood everything without saying a word, just for his sake, and for their sakes has never mentioned the immeasurable distance which separates them from her!*

"I don't know why I write all this to you, I, who never talk to any one about myself; but I think it will make little difference to you, as you are in the habit of listening to people's confidence, while to me it does make a difference. When one keeps one's feelings pent up so long one gets bitter, oh, so bitter, that it frightens one. I have fought against this, and keep on fighting. I am so young and I want to be happy. I try to think of the future, of more cheerful days, making imaginary plans for a little home, beautiful and refined, peaceful and sweet, for my baby boy to grow up in, but something in me keeps on crying: What's the use of hoping that way; who was ever known to be happy in this world! Oh, how much I want to be happy."

Ask John de Saulles to punt a football, run with it thirty yards, or dodge an onrush of line backers trying to tackle him, and he would not blink. Ask him to nurture a young, lonely weeping girl, and he is utterly lost. John had expected his adoring wife to feel overjoyed at bringing his son into the world. He might have wondered what went wrong with the fun-loving, dancing girl he had married just a year before. She just wanted to cry, or pout, and would not (or could not) articulate what made her so unhappy. Never in his life had he known a girl that he could not cheer up with a joke, a kiss, or a tickle in the ribs. If he tried too hard to make her laugh against her will, she reacted physically—a girlish slap or a weak shove. Her impenetrable depression wounded his masculine pride, baffled and confused him. This was one game he could not win by tackling someone into the muddy grass.

Grecian Urns

We don't dance with our hearts.

BLANCA DE SAULLES

John removed Blanca from his parents' home and provided a cottage for her and their son at the luxury community of Deal Beach, New Jersey. This was his first attempt at making a real home since arriving in the United States a year before. Even so, John still spent most of his time in New York City working real estate deals to support his family. Blanca stayed alone in the cottage with a few servants who were like strangers underfoot. They helped her with the baby, they made her toast and coffee in the morning, but she did not bond with any of them as friends.

When he made the commute from New York City on the weekends, John brought his friend Marshall E. Ward—a financier and stock broker—tagging along to talk business over supper and cigars. The lawsuit with the Paul J. Rainey Company now a settled matter, the two men were the best of friends. However, Blanca did not get along with Marshall and apparently the feeling was mutual. She resented a third person in the house, a male friend who usurped the precious time that she hoped to spend with her husband. While she sat alone by the baby's cradle upstairs, the two men shared hours together drinking, smoking, and talking in leather armchairs by the fire.

89

The cottage location did not solve their marital problems or make her happy the way John had hoped. Blanca suffered in the humidity and crushing heat of summertime in the Northeast, a climate radically different from the refreshing sea breezes of Viña del Mar. In late August 1913, she collapsed with an attack of heatstroke and had to recover at a hospital.[69]

With luxury also came isolation. Before the days of burglar alarms and video surveillance cameras, the homes of the rich and famous were prime targets for burglars. As a gift, and for personal security, John bought his wife a Smith & Wesson revolver for self-protection and taught her how to use it.

At the turn of the 20th century, it became socially acceptable for upper-class women to own and shoot guns. The sharpshooter Annie Oakley, after her retirement from Buffalo Bill's Wild West Show, gave shooting lessons to groups of polite women as late as the 1920s. Improvements in gun design also made firearms easier to handle, load, and fire. Lighter weight handguns, rifles, and fashionable shooting attire were marketed to women. It was a fad for wealthy Americans to go to gun clubs for target practice and sport hunting. Ladies participated in shooting alongside their fathers, boyfriends, or husbands.

John and Blanca followed the trend and sometimes went target shooting together at the country club. They both became excellent marksmen.[70] He had been an accomplished shooter for years, a hobby that he shared with his friend and former business partner Paul J. Rainey although John had never traveled along with Rainey on one of his African lion hunting expeditions. At the country club's fenced-in shooting range, John and Blanca side by side practiced aiming pistols at bulls-eyes and clay pigeons. She would later use this same gifted Smith & Wesson to kill him.

The weather cooled, and another snowy winter darkened the coast. In December of 1913, they celebrated their second anniversary and, a few weeks later, little Jack passed his first birthday on Christmas Day. The active child was able to stand up and attempted a few stumbling steps around the twinkling tinsel garlands on the evergreen tree.

In the early months of 1914, John found a way to turn back the clock and re-set the last 10 years of his life. He fell in with a pack of thirty-ish men from the exclusive gentlemen's clubs in New York City. They formed the Interclub Baseball League and competed for a pennant of their own design. The games were not sponsored by anyone but themselves--wealthy businessmen and weekend athletes eager to prove that they were not old yet. John's buddy Arthur Barnwell, from the Yale baseball team, played umpire. John joined the Union Club's team and the five other teams came from the University Club, the Racquet and Tennis

Club, the Knickerbocker Club, the Calumet Club, and the Twelfth Infantry Regiment. The baseball teams in previous years had knocked balls around a vacant lot at 31st Street and Madison Avenue, but this year they moved uptown to an empty corner of Fifth Ave and 72nd Street owned by W.K. Vanderbilt.

The Interclub Baseball League provided the only outdoor ball games in the winter season. In other words, no one else was this crazy.

The *New York Times* was curious enough to send reporters out there, in double layers of wool coats and ear muffs, to watch the daredevils playing baseball in the snow. In diligent newspaper fashion, they recorded the scores and a play-by-play of the games. As these men were the *crème de la crème* of has-beens, they put on a good show. John de Saulles on third base demonstrated that he still had the right stuff, "playing in his most spectacular style, in grabbing fly balls off the outfield nets and armory walls."[71] The self-imposed baseball season continued until May 1914 when the University Club captured the pennant in a very close score of 10 to 9. John's team from the Union Club came in second place. Their loss was nothing to be ashamed of, as John's team had put in a great effort. "Tilt was on second base when Jack de Saulles, the old Yale quarterback, smashed out a long double. Tilt ran in from second and was crossing the plate when Homan's throw hit him, retiring the side. Had Tilt scored, the score would have been tied."[72]

❧❧

At the same time John was knocking out double plays and sliding into home plate, Blanca participated in a grand society function at the Waldorf-Astoria hotel at its historic location on 5th Avenue before it would be demolished in 1931 to make way for the Empire State building. Easter week in April 1914 was the season for charity balls, and the crème of New York's social aristocracy competed to out-do each other in *noblesse oblige.* Proceeds of another masque ball went to St. Mark's Hospital. A grand *fete* over at the Hotel Astor benefited the New York Association for the Blind with patrons including President Wilson, Governor Glynn, and ambassadors of several European countries. Everybody who was anybody in society circles just had to be at one or more of these splendid events, as much to donate to charity as to show off their designer ball gowns and exotic feathered hats.

The *New York Tribune* called the *fete* at the Waldorf-Astoria the premier society event of Easter week and listed the names of ticketed attendees across several columns of the newspaper.[73] John and Blanca de Saulles were among the local celebrities. Benefits would go to the Loomis Sanatorium Annex to purchase beds for tuberculosis patients—a very personal cause to Blanca considering her own father had died of the disease.

A twittering committee of high-society ladies organized the entertainment, the main feature being a *tableaux.*

Tableaux vivant, a French term for "living picture," was a popular form of performance art in the 19th century. A group of costumed models arrange themselves in choreographed poses set against elaborate stage backgrounds with dramatic lighting and musical accompaniment. For the duration of the display, the models do not speak or move. Themes for tableaux range from reproducing famous works of Renaissance art (Leonardo da Vinci's Last Supper is a favorite) and scenes of Bible stories. Sometimes the more *avant-garde* performers in Europe challenged Victorian censorship with presentations of semi-nude women portraying characters from Ancient Greek myths.

Blanca de Saulles struck a pose in a costume of satin, organdy, and chiffon, along with seven other ladies of society fame. She powdered her face to whiten her olive complexion that, even with a winter spent indoors, appeared darker than the fair-haired maidens gathering on stage with her. By her left hand, Louise Heckscher (the wife of John's cousin Maurice) fixed her gaze on the lofty chandelier and held still. One by one, the living statues made their stately march onto the stage. Three other married women and three single girls completed the scene.[74] Arms aloft and hands drooped like a ballet frozen in time, the eight ladies remained stoic—unmoving and unmoved. Cellos moaned out a soft refrain over the arpeggios tinkling like wind chimes out of a grand piano.

John de Saulles and his cousin Maurice Heckscher, as the gentlemen's floor committee, stood by uncomfortably trussed in tuxedos, bow ties, and starched collars. I imagine that John perked up when the scaled-down brass band struck up a lively beat. Saxophones with a raunchy voice replaced the stately cellos. Trumpets tooted. Marching drums shaped like tambourines tapped out a rapid cadence. Piano keyboards took on a new life as wiggling fingers tickled out a syncopated rhythm. Irving Berlin and Scott Joplin tunes echoed the faster pace of the city streets outside—a nighttime that whirred of trolleys, trains, automobiles, and steamships. The graceful, rigid ladies of the *tableaux* departed stage left to make way for modern dancers.

Couples in sassy sleeveless dresses and beige striped suits, arm in arm, skipped around in demonstration of a Pavlova gavotte, a fancy one-step, and the maxixe heel step. Victorian society was falling away like icicles melting from the eaves of the hotel's façade, and the prudish dances of his father's generation—the waltz and the box step—were being replaced. No longer did dancing partners have to hold each other at arms' length. Under the pretext of dance costume, women got away with revealing bare arms and ankles, but still had a long way to go to become "flappers." The Argentine tango was a scandalous dance that no polite society woman would admit to knowing. Called a vertical expression of a horizontal activity, the tango would later sweep the nation when introduced later by Rudolph Valentino in a 1920 silent film. But back in 1914, when everyone was still a bit innocent, couples dancing the *maxixe* kept a polite three inches of distance.

The *maxixe* heel step was the specialty of Joan Sawyer, an up-and-coming exhibition ballroom dancer, who would later play a pivotal role in the lives of John and Blanca. She published dance instructions in women's magazines for those ladies who were too scandalized to go to the Ziegfeld Follies to see the latest ragtime steps for themselves. A self-made businesswoman and outspoken suffragette, she created an innovative female-centered sheikdom in New York with her Persian Garden lounge. She employed an orchestra of genuine African-American musicians, not white men painted in minstrel black face, led by Jamaican-born Dan Kildare.

Another guest on the party list was John's cousin Captain Philip M. Lydig, the son of John's aunt Pauline Heckscher Lydig. About ten years older than John, the captain cut quite a dashing figure in a tuxedo and top hat. He wore society fashions with an air of authority, a military poise, the kind of grace that came with going "there" and coming back alive. A graduate of Harvard, he had earned his rank during service in the Spanish-American War, and since returning to civilian life in 1899 had prospered as a banker with the New York Stock Exchange.[75] John admired his cousin's distinguished military background and socialized with him at the Union Club where they were both members.

Perhaps Blanca felt an affinity with Captain Lydig, more than the other Heckscher relatives, because he had married a Latina. The captain's wife Rita de Alba de Acosta was a famously beautiful woman, the subject of several artistic portraits, and a glamorous society butterfly. For that one night, Captain Lydig kept his shameful secret private from the party-goers and the tabloids: his glamorous society marriage was disintegrating. His wife was not on a holiday; Rita had left him, for good, and they would be officially divorced in Paris a few years later.

❧❧

President Woodrow Wilson nominated John in March 1914 to be foreign minister to Uruguay.[76] The national newspapers hyped the honor, and Blanca was excited for more personal reasons than her husband's glory. Uruguay is on the east coast of South America, near the Argentine city of Buenos Aires, and the newly constructed Transandine Railroad made a direct horizontal line connecting back to Santiago, Chile. Her hopes inflated to imagine herself with her husband and her toddling son living once more in a Latin country. She could almost hear the church bells of Viña del Mar ringing in the distance.

John de Saulles wrote a letter of thanks to Colonel House, on March 19, 1914,[77] to say:

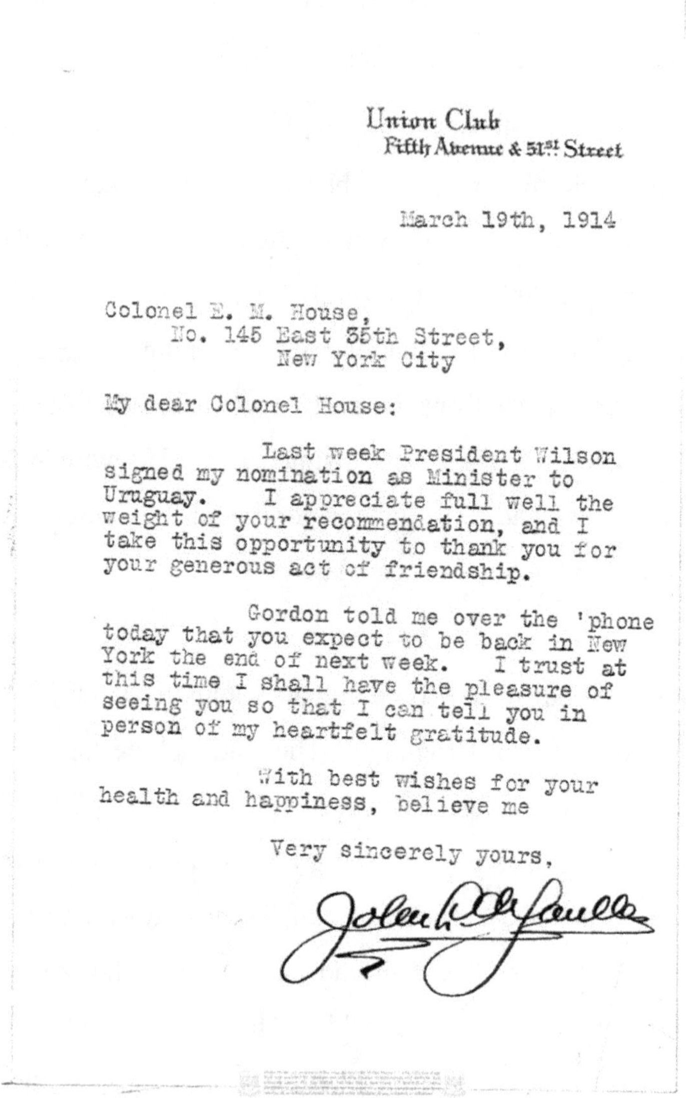

Union Club
Fifth Avenue & 51st Street

March 19th, 1914

Colonel E. M. House,
    No. 145 East 35th Street,
        New York City

My dear Colonel House:

          Last week President Wilson signed my nomination as Minister to Uruguay. I appreciate full well the weight of your recommendation, and I take this opportunity to thank you for your generous act of friendship.

          Gordon told me over the 'phone today that you expect to be back in New York the end of next week. I trust at this time I shall have the pleasure of seeing you so that I can tell you in person of my heartfelt gratitude.

          With best wishes for your health and happiness, believe me

          Very sincerely yours,

          John L. de Saulles

Fig. 15 - John L. de Saulles personal letter to Colonel Edward Mandell House

Apparently he and Blanca kept separate residences, with John staying temporarily in New York City to conduct his business affairs. Colonel House replied on March 25, 1914, addressed to John at the Union Club, "You have no friend who is better pleased over your appointment than I and I hope you will call some day before you sail in order to give me the pleasure of congratulating you in person. I am sure you will be a credit to your friends, to the Administration and to your country."

Blanca also wrote a letter to John around this time, to tell him of a telephone call she received from President Wilson's personal secretary Joseph Tumulty.[78] "I have tried to get you on the phone this afternoon, but when I called up, you were absent from the club. Lester Jones called up and he said everything looked most cheerful and that Tumulty wanted to see you either Tuesday, Wednesday, or Thursday in the morning; he told Tumulty to wire you, which he did, and I am enclosing the wire; also a letter from L. J. which came this morning just after you phoned. I opened it, thinking there might be something of importance in it, but did not think it worth while to phone it to you. You can judge for yourself. I hope you are well and are taking good care of yourself. I am ever so much better and am looking forward with great pleasure to your return. We might go to N.Y. together on Monday and then you go on to Washington either that night or Tuesday, and I return here, tho' I should simply love to go with you except I might be in your way. Toodles is very well and everything is as it has been." On the margin of this letter she wrote, "*Where were you????*" with four exclamation marks.

John was among several guest speakers at a Saturday luncheon of the Republican Club, the topic being the best ways to improve Latin American and United States relations. Addressing the crowd, John spoke of a need for American banks and merchant marines in South America, but most importantly, a good daily news service to keep the people informed about one another. In his opinion, much of the misunderstandings came from inaccurate reports in the press. The ex-attorney general George Wickersham recommended more educational programs and the U.S. government's support of investors to foster trade between the two regions.

Also at the luncheon, the Costa Rican Consul General Manuel Gonzalez Zeledon laid the blame entirely on the United States and gave an earful to the gathering. His poignant speech is as valid today as it was 100 years ago. "When you want anything... you go and get it. You haven't wanted to understand the Latin Americans and so you don't understand them... You don't understand our language. When Latin Americans come here you want them to speak English, and when you go to their countries if they don't talk English to you, you have nothing to do with them....

Go to them and find out what they think, and, most of all, find out what they love. They love their countries and they love liberty. Don't disturb them in this love. Keep your hands off of their governments." [79]

Sometime in May 1914, Blanca decided that she had been stuck in the United States for long enough. She traveled abroad with a fellow Chilean friend, Miss Muñoz, and brought her son little Jack along on a trip to Europe.[80] Before she departed, John asked to borrow $37,000 from her personal inheritance for the purpose of securing the Uruguay appointment. Blanca later said at her murder trial that he squandered it all instead on gambling and cabaret dancers, but we only have her word for this.

Two months later, John stunned everyone when he publicly turned down the president's offer to be Minister to Uruguay.[81] John made a special trip to Washington D.C. to hand in his resignation to the Secretary of State after he had already taken the oath of office.[82] He wrote a personal letter to Colonel House,[83] offering his thanks and appreciation while apologizing for withdrawing from the role.

Union Club
Fifth Avenue & 51st Street

June 3rd, 1914

My dear Mr. House:

Circumstances have arisen
which prevent me from going to Uruguay as
Minister, and I have handed my resignation
to the Secretary of State and explained
to him that nothing except added responsibilities of the greatest importance would
have prevented me from accepting the great
honor conferred upon me by President
Wilson and the Senate of the United States.

I am writing you this letter
as I want you to know my appreciation
of the kindly interest you took in my
behalf at the time when I thought it
would be possible for me to serve my
country in a foreign land.

I take this opportunity to
thank you once more for the friendship
you displayed toward me.

Believe me

Most sincerely,

To: Colonel E. M. House,
         No. 145 East 35th St.,
         New York City

Fig. 16 - John L. de Saulles personal letter to Colonel Edward Mandell House

In the early days of his administration, President Wilson struggled to fill the seats of foreign consulates. John was not the only man to refuse a diplomatic post. One after another, the highly qualified men he approached turned him down and Wilson's bottom-of-the-list choices served in Great Britain and Germany at the outbreak of World War One in Europe.

Fig. 17 - Col. Edward Mandell House with President Woodrow Wilson (1915)

Whatever personal reasons John had for resigning from the Uruguay post remain a mystery. He did not explain himself to Blanca as she was away in England when he made his decision. At her murder trial she speculated that he had greedy ambitions to

103

multiply his wealth and a diplomatic appointment was not as lucrative. Although it is plausible, John seems the type to be more interested in the things that money can buy rather than money itself. He fully understood the honor of the appointment, and he had to realize that by resigning at the last minute, he was burning a bridge that could not be rebuilt. Wilson reached out his hand to John de Saulles twice, and both times he had been refused. John would never again be nominated for any other position in Wilson's administration.

Heckscher & de Saulles

*The more I go out and the more men I meet,
the greater is my thankfulness that I belong to you.*

BLANCA DE SAULLES

John went into partnership in a real estate company with his cousin on his mother's side. G. Maurice Heckscher was the only son of millionaire philanthropist August Heckscher. One has to wonder how much of this partnership was John's original idea and how much was prodding by the elder Mr. Heckscher. Not only did Maurice play polo skillfully at Long Island country clubs, but he enjoyed playing daredevil as a recreational pilot of early aircraft over the same grassy plains where the Wright Brothers sometimes came to test their designs. He owned an amphibious craft (the Curtiss Flying Boat) that carried his gleeful grin soaring over the waters of Long Island Sound. Wearing flight goggles and a leather cap, he could lean out from the cockpit and wave to his stern father as he buzzed overhead of old Mr. Heckscher's yacht. In a few short years, during World War One, airplanes would become a serious business and military aviators would train for combat over these Long Island plains. But in 1915, aircraft were thrilling toys for rich playboys wasting their inheritance. The senior cousin John de Saulles was called upon to play quarterback and bring Maurice's feet literally back down to earth. Maurice also had family obligations with a lovely wife—society belle Louise Vanderhoef—

and a trio of toddling children to support. The son of a millionaire could not afford to be a failure in life, no matter what.

Fig. 18 - G.M. Heckscher's "Curtiss Flying Boat"

As August Heckscher explained in Forbes' book *Men Who Are Making America*, "The trouble with most Americans who fail to succeed is not that they are not brilliant enough, but because they have not laid the proper foundation. They are not thorough enough. They do not master their subject from the ground up. They dislike the tediousness, the study, and the labour involved in laying foundations. They do not want to begin at the bottom—they seem to forget that men like Lincoln and Washington did not start at the top and that Napoleon began as an obscure artillery officer. You must learn to obey before you are fit to command."[84]

The newly formed venture of Heckscher & de Saulles returned John to the world he had known five years before in the days when he had built the Nassau Hotel and managed other high-end properties. He got involved with August Heckscher's plans to build a new sort of modern building, called a skyscraper, that would transform New York's silhouette. Bethlehem Steel provided the girders and crossbeams for the buildings rising higher and higher every day. In a couple of years, when completed in 1916, the Heckscher Building in downtown Manhattan would be one of the first impressive towers of a modern New York city skyline. Shortly before he was killed, John de Saulles personally managed leasing a few of the Heckscher Building's exclusive offices.

Fig. 19 - The Heckscher building at 5th Avenue & 57th Street, New York City, circa 1921, with Cornelius Vanderbilt's home in the foreground

That summer of 1914, John bought a four-story luxury townhouse at 22 East 78th Street on the upper east side of Manhattan between Fifth and Madison Avenues.[85] He lived the solitary life of a bachelor but he was never really alone. A house staff cooked and cleaned for him. A Chinese laundry starched his white collars. Shoeshine boys by the newsstand buffed his leather loafers. Each day, he paid two pennies for the morning paper and got a clean shave at the local barber shop. A chauffeur drove him around the city in the latest model automobiles. Secretaries in his real estate office took dictation and transferred his words on small black typewriters. He enjoyed business lunches at swanky downtown restaurants, and in the afternoons puffed cigars at the gentlemen's clubs. He negotiated the sales of high-end real estate properties with iced cocktails and smiles and handshakes. Most evenings found him dining at ritzy supper clubs, like Delmonico's and Sherry's, where a single meal cost as much as his secretary's monthly salary.

Though he was not a dancer himself, John de Saulles attracted beautiful showgirls to hang on his arm at Joan Sawyer's Persian Garden and at Broadway's Ziegfield Follies. Fast-paced ragtime music energized the nights at rooftop cabarets overlooking the electric streetlights of the city. A popular Irving Berlin song from a few years before says it best: *"My wife's gone to th' country.*

Hurrah, hurrah! She thought it best, I need a rest, that's why she went away. She took the children with her. Hurrah, hurrah!"

Blanca and little Jack Jr. stayed away vacationing in Europe for the whole spring and summer of 1914. She took a nanny to care for the baby, a 36-year old Irish spinster Anne Mooney nicknamed "Booby" by little Jack. She socialized with her newlywed brother Billy Errázuriz and his wife Maria Edwards in the classy circles that even the New York's social register envied. Blanca had other relatives living in France, also.

Her uncle José Tomas Errázuriz had been a distinguished artist at the *Academia de Pintura* (Academy of Painting) in Santiago, Chile. He spent all of his adult life in Europe pursuing his talent as a landscape artist in the realistic style in contrast to the *avant-garde* experimentation of his contemporaries Gaugin, Degas, and Van Gogh. He was not interested in making money and rarely sold a piece of art in his lifetime; he donated most of his works to charity. His wife Eugenie Errázuriz exhibited grace and fashionable style in European social circles, her gowns and hats as elegant and tasteful as her no-frills style of interior decorating. She developed a motto, "Elegance means elimination," and is known as one of the originators of the minimalist aesthetic. She hung curtains of unlined linen, whitewashed her interior walls like a peasant's cottage, had no carpets, and detested knick-knacks. It is said that she washed her hair in rain water. "A house that does not alter," she liked to say, "is a dead house."[86] Eugenie's *joie de vivre* shines in several oil portraits by such renowned artists as John Singer Sergeant and a young Pablo Picasso who adored her.

Fig. 20 - Portrait of Eugenia Huici Arguedas de Errázuriz, in Paris, by Jacques-Emile Blanche (1890)

Another of Blanca's aunts, Amalia Errázuriz, had married Ramon Subercaseaux Vicuña who served as the Chilean ambassador to France. A lovely woman with a delicate frame and pensive dark eyes, Amalia posed for portraits painted by such renowned artists as Boldini and John Singer Sergeant. Theirs was a world of white dresses with ruffled skirts, pearl necklaces, and gondola rides on the River Seine to be captured in oil pastels. In later years, Blanca visited her aunt's home in Paris and enjoyed the

110

cultured refrains of Chopin and Debussy played on a grand piano. It was a glamorous lifestyle of Impressionist watercolors and classical opera that Blanca always aspired to have but would never achieve in her marriage with John.

She nibbled at light meals in Paris bistros and drank coffee after dark to give her energy to dance for hours at tango tea parlors. Blanca wrote John a letter that illustrates her ability to have a good time without him. Dated June 29, 1914, addressed to "Dearest, Darling Dinky," her letter says,[87]

> *"You have no idea how I enjoyed your perfectly wonderful letters. One of them specially has made me so glad that I look forward immensely to returning to my home which is you. Dinky, you need not be afraid that I shall regret having married you. On the contrary, the more I go out and the more men I meet, the greater is my thankfulness that I belong to you. Dinky, I know I'm horribly selfish to be off by myself having a good time, and to have taken Toodle away from you, but you will forgive me, won't you, and think that I'm very young, and that all my friends in New York were so old, the youngest being dear old Louise, who was a woman of 30 when your wife was only 19. Here I have been mostly with girls and boys of my own age, people to whom life is still a rosy dream, and not so frightfully real and earnest as it becomes to those who have passed their first youth.*
>
> *"I am playing in the sunshine, forgetful of everything save the joy of living. I feel so young and cheerful, and I have such a wonderful feeling in my heart, that at the slightest sign of weariness, or*

111

*should any clouds disturb my sunshine, I have you
to go back to and your strong arms to hold me. Oh,
Dinky, it will be such a wonderful homecoming for
me, and I'm so glad I came away, because I've
learned to appreciate you and your goodness. I
shall be so glad to settle down in our little home,
and won't we be happy in it! Dinky, it will be too
wonderful!*

*"You wrote an awfully sweet letter to Auntie, but it
has upset me frightfully to think you are worried
about me—don't you trust me any more? You seem
to be afraid suddenly that some one will run away
with me. Jack, if you don't believe me loyal, at least
give me the credit of having a very good head on my
shoulders, and a good insight into characters. I am
exceedingly careful as to whose invitations I accept
and whose I refuse, and I always know when I can
go out with a man.*

*"By the way, I saw Elsie Janis at the Palace. She is
scoring an immense success. You will be glad to
hear Ostend appeals to me strongly—the bathing,
the casino, lots of dancing, the races, &c. They still
gamble there, but that doesn't make any difference
to me. I have vague ambitions to run down to
Biarritz for one week. There are crowds of people
going that I know, and several people have begged
me to go. That would be in August, before going
back. I shall try to persuade Billy and Maria to go
as chaperons, if I have any money left by that time."*

Blanca finished up her vacation when she ran out of money.
She sailed out from Southampton, England and returned to New
York on August 5, 1914, along the same route where the *Titanic*

had sunk among the icebergs just two years before. The Ellis Island arrival records show that she brought the Irish nanny Anne Mooney back to New York as well. Her toddling son was almost two years old, walking more steadily, growing fast, eating solid foods, learning his first words. She took up residence with John in the townhouse on East 78th Street and suffered through the end of another hot, humid New York summer.

Fig. 21 - John de Saulles and his son

A studio portrait photograph shows John de Saulles in a stylish suit and straw hat, holding the hand of his son little Jack who wears a white sailor's costume.

113

Portraits taken by the photographer Arnold Genthe portray Blanca alone in glamorous poses wearing a dark chiffon tea gown. She is strikingly gorgeous at age twenty, the hardships of motherhood fading away before the lens of a camera. Her unshakable melancholy gives her expression a faraway, ethereal stare. In all my research, I am unable to find a photograph of John and Blanca together.

England's Ninth Duke of Manchester became friends with John de Saulles around this time. They met while negotiating a contract to furnish thousands of horses to the Canadian military.[88] Roughly the same age as John, in his mid-thirties, the duke was a rakish fellow named William Montagu who had succeeded his father to the dukedom in 1892 at the age of 15 and held a seat on the Liberals bench in the House of Lords. Although married and a father of four little children, the duke was a notorious spender often traveling the world to avoid creditors while having a jolly good time for himself. John's mother Catherine once asked Blanca to intervene and try to end their friendship[89] after seeing an article in *Town Topics* that described an intoxicated young girl falling overboard during a wild party on the duke's yacht.

Blanca would complain later, at the murder trial, of a scandalous occasion while visiting the Heckscher cousins on their luxury yacht. The stately August Heckscher enjoyed calling himself a commodore when he sailed mini-voyages in the mild waters of Long Island Sound. The Duke of Manchester's yacht glided by—two ships passing in broad daylight—with John and a gaggle of Broadway beauties surrounding him on the breezy deck. Scandalous women, who wore V-necks in the daytime! Blanca was properly mortified and affronted.

The Duke of Manchester incorporated several motion picture companies that year. The largest venture was the International Educational League with capital stocks of $10 million, for the purpose of supplying the world with "motion picture films of an historic, educational, scientific and other character."[90] He leased an apartment at No. 4 West 57th Street[91] and began remodeling the interior to suit his preferences. He shipped over from England many of his own rare tapestries and paintings. However, two months later, his motion picture enterprise went belly-up and the duke sold all his assets at auction—down to his office furniture—to raise cash for creditors.[92]

Blanca accused John of spending all his free time at Broadway theaters and cabaret restaurants, carrying on with silent film actresses and ballroom dancers like Bonnie Glass and Joan Sawyer. She testified at her murder trial about finding receipts in his pockets for women's gifts. She told the sympathetic jury that her husband often staggered home drunk and passed out on the living room sofa, if he came home at all.

Their final showdown began when John took a business trip to Europe. He departed the U.S. in the last week of October and traveled to London, arriving on November 5, 1914 to stay at the luxurious Bentley Hotel. It appears that John intended to stay abroad for a while, and in London applied at the embassy for traveling papers to go back and forth between France and England for a period of up to two years, returning to the U.S. "eventually." The passport photograph shows him looking very sharp and respectable in a suit.

Blanca applied for a passport on November 23, 1914 with a handwritten notation to rush the processing because she would sail on Wednesday the 25th. Her signature, in contrast to John's large stylish sweeps of the pen, is tightly written, rigid and controlled. Her passport was issued just in time, and she hopped aboard the steamship *Adriatic*. After a week on rough gray seas, she chugged into Liverpool on a cold gray day December 3, 1914.

The way she told the story at her trial[93], Blanca arrived at the Bentley Hotel and announced herself to the desk clerk as his wife. The clerk responded, "Which one?" implying that his hotel room had a revolving door for anonymous women. As further insult, John apparently refused to allow her to share the room at the Bentley, saying that it was his business headquarters. Thus rejected, and with the hotel fully booked, she found a room elsewhere at the

116

historic Cadogan Hotel nearby. Blanca later harped on the shame and disgrace she felt, not only a personal insult but an embarrassment in the eyes of her society friends. What loving husband turns his wife out on the street after she sailed the ocean to be at his side?

Overlapping with John's and Blanca's travels, his brother Charles de Saulles applied in New York for a passport on November 5, 1914—the same day of John's arrival in London. Charles sailed aboard the *Lapland* and arrived in Liverpool, England on November 19, 1914. He did not bring his wife and two children on this trip, either; it was not a holiday. He stayed in Europe for about a month, conducting business as a metallurgical engineer for the American Smelting & Refining Company with offices in Manhattan. The Guggenheim family, copper tycoons, owned a large share of this company and at this time they engaged in a large volume business. Copper mined in Chile and refined in the U.S. was shipped as ingots to Europe, and the Guggenheims prospered greatly off the profits. I have no information on whether John's international business ventures related to his brother's or if it was a coincidence of timing. Charles de Saulles soon returned to New York on December 12, 1914 separately from his brother.

Shortly after his wife's arrival in December, John departed from London for Paris and points beyond. As Blanca told it later, John rejected her tender affections by not allowing her to join him on a trip to the continent. The anecdote told at her murder trial was an example of him being a cold-hearted, neglectful husband. On the other hand, looking at the political timeline, it was not very wise for her to wish to go with him. The most intense fighting of World War One, to date, was at the Battle of Marne in early September 1914, when the French army managed to hold off the German advance. The French stood their ground and declared, "They shall not pass!" (*"On ne passe pas!"*) From that point on, the farm fields of France turned into a maze of trenches and barbed wire; cannons boomed day and night; whole villages evacuated. If Blanca had romantic notions of shopping for hats in Paris, or having coffee and cookies under the striped awnings of a bistro, she would have found a very different city at that time. Paris was on lockdown, braced for a German invasion. The actress Elsie Janis, also touring in Paris around this time, described in her autobiography the nightly air raids of German biplanes dropping bombs at random targets in the city. Young men were not interested in dancing at cabarets anymore; they were donning uniforms to go to the trenches. If John told her to remain in London or to go home to New York, it was the most sensible thing he could say to her.

They spent their third anniversary, December 14, 1914, in separate cities, separate countries, and separate realities.

While in London, she made the acquaintance of a Mr. Harold Fowler.[94] By some accounts, John had introduced his wife to Fowler at a society function or business dinner. Blanca dined with him, danced the fox-trot with him, and tried to forget her sorrows in the company of a man younger than her husband. Born in Liverpool to globe-trotting U.S. citizens, Fowler had spent his later childhood in New York and attended Columbia University. He was a partner in the financial firm of White, Weld & Co. and in 1913 was invited to become the secretary of the U.S. Ambassador to Great Britain Walter Hines Page (an appointee of President Wilson).[95] When the war broke out in August 1914, Fowler applied to the British Army but was not accepted right away; he would be able to serve later, but at this time, he was a young single man frustrated to still be a civilian.

Blanca returned to the U.S. on December 23, 1914, without her husband, on the same steamship (the *Lusitania*) with Harold Fowler. They are listed on the same page of the arriving passenger manifest list, which means they walked the gangplank almost side by side. Blanca in a stylish hat and fur coat smiled and condescendingly flattered the customs official who met her at the dock. The officer said, "It isn't always we have such a passenger as you, and although we all know who Mrs. de Saulles is, we have not the honor of knowing you."

According to Blanca, in a letter to John written shortly afterwards, "It was bitterly cold and we had to wait some time for my case of silver to come out of the hold. So I said it was a shame he had to wait so much, and he answered that he would not mind waiting every day of his life, if he were to see me. So I said I would not mind arriving every day, if I could see him. The result was that everything was expedited—no questions asked. I shook hands when I said good-bye. I told him he must come to see us, &c., &c., &c. Of course he was in the seventh heaven of delight. You know better than anyone what saying that means to people of that class. It was all very amusing and very useful."[96]

After landing in New York, she continued to see Harold Fowler socially. He worked in New York city in the financial district and on the weekends aspired to be an aviator. Perhaps he made friends with Maurice Heckscher and weather permitting begged a ride in the Curtiss Flying Boat soaring over the grassy beaches of Long Island. Blanca de Saulles would be in Harold Fowler's company, not her husband's, for Christmas Day (her son's second birthday) and for New Year's Eve.

On January 3, 1915, Blanca wrote a letter to John—who was still in Europe—to inform him about attending a party with Maurice Heckscher, his wife Louise, and her new acquaintance. "My Darling Dink: This is the first letter I write this year, and the first wish is for your welfare and your success. I think of you all the time, and am so anxious to know how you are getting on. You are a lazy Dink—you ought to write to your wife. New Year's night we went to the first Friday evening dance, and we missed you dreadfully. Maurice was feeling splendidly. He came off the wagon for the occasion. Louise and I had every one at our feet, and we danced till we had none left to stand on. Fowler went with us." [97]

Four months later, John de Saulles sailed home alone to New York on the *Lusitania* on April 24, 1915 just a few weeks before the luxury steamship would be torpedoed and sunk by a German submarine. That incident of an unprovoked attack on a civilian ship outraged the United States, as much as the September 11, 2001 attack on the World Trade Center, and would lay the groundwork for President Wilson to abandon his policy of neutrality and urge Congress to join the fight in World War One. The *Lusitania* tragedy was more personal for John, as he saw his own marriage sinking beyond hope. Sometime after the luxury steamship went down, John said to friends that he wished he had drowned on it.[98]

Oceans Between

*I adored her. She seemed so far above me
that I never dreamed she would look at a mere tango dancer*

RUDOLPH VALENTINO
SILENT FILM STAR

The day after returning to New York in April 1915, John de Saulles joined in a ball game with his buddies at the Interclub Baseball League on the vacant lot at 72nd Street and Fifth Avenue. This time, he played for the Knickerbocker Club's team and the newspaper credits his batting and outfielder skills with contributing to victory.

Yet his prowess on the baseball diamond did not translate into teamwork at home. This is the time they supposedly had an argument that resulted in a heart to heart discussion of their situation. According to Blanca, John admitted that he was not interested in being a married man or settling down, that he preferred the bachelor life of drinking and partying with Broadway beauties. On the other hand, there may be more to her relationship with Harold Fowler than anyone can ever know. She admitted at her murder trial of socializing with him, but whether or not they had an affair became a moot point. By this time, Fowler had left for England to serve in the Royal Field Artillery.

John offered her a divorce, but she resisted the idea. Society at that time considered divorce to be the ultimate scandal.

A woman's identity ceased to be her own upon marriage. Blanca had been Mrs. John Longer de Saulles for almost four years, and if her marriage ended she would be reduced to an anonymous divorcée. Blanca's personal objections ran even deeper. Being a Roman Catholic, divorce was considered to be a sin; what God had joined no human court had the authority to dissolve. Before the reforms of the Vatican II council in the early 1960s, a divorced person was entirely shunned. She would be disgraced in her soul before God, the Virgin Mary, and all the saints.

Instead of choosing a divorce, she simply picked up little Jack and abandoned her husband to return to Chile to be with her mother. Her good-bye letter, addressed to "Dear Jack" was read aloud by the prosecutor at her murder trial. Curiously, it has the tone of an apology, not what you would expect from a woman angry at a drunkard, cheating husband. This does not seem to be a passive enabler making excuses for her husband's behavior but someone who has done some unspecified wrong. The prosecutor who poked at the issues was unable to crack Blanca's cool composure on the witness stand; we will never know what she really meant in begging his forgiveness.

> *"Just before leaving I want to tell you that I am really sorry for having made you so unhappy, and I want you to please forgive me, and realize that if I hurt you it was always unconsciously. I know,*

though, that no excuse makes it any better; a hurt is a hurt. But I want you to know that I have always been fond of you and admired you as a man among men, and nothing will ever change that. That I was not able to make a good wife will ever be a regret to me and a source of reproach. Circumstances and people change so much that who knows that some day, if you wanted still, we might be happy. However, I feel as though you do not like me, and will never want to see me again, and, though I justly deserve it, it does hurt, because, as I say, I am very fond of you and shall always be tremendously interested in all your doings, and hope from the bottom of my heart that you will find the happiness which is your due. As long as I have Toodie I shall make a good mother to him, and make him look forward to the time he will see you again." [99]

July 1915 brought the autumn season in Chile, and although the weather turned cooler Blanca's spirits found solace in the soft breezes wafting off the hillside vineyards. She cried it all out on her mother's and sister's sympathetic shoulders. All her old friends in Viña del Mar agreed that *norteamericanos,* in general, were terrible husbands.

A whole year passed with John and Blanca living on separate continents, on opposite hemispheres of the globe. He continued to live alone in the townhouse on East 78th Street. In his free time, John volunteered in the service of customs inspector Dudley Field Malone and accompanied him in boarding German vessels seized in the New York harbor. [100] Branching out from the real estate market, John and Maurice Heckscher entered into a new business venture.[101] The American Spelter Corporation, started in October 27, 1915, marketed the raw material synonymous for zinc or zinc alloys. The company did not own its own mines but bought ores in the open market and redistributed the product under contract. John de Saulles was president, Maurice the vice-president, and a minerals specialist named George Nicholson was treasurer and general manager.

In Chile, Blanca suffered an automobile crash but recovered in time to celebrate Christmas 1915 and her son's third birthday at home in Viña del Mar with her mother and her sister. Perhaps her brother Billy and his wife Maria came home to visit too. A bright warm sun shined over Christmas at the Palacio Vergara, so different from the dark snowy days in Pennsylvania. At that moment, she never intended to go back.

John played baseball with the Interclub League for the last time in early 1916. They had lost the use of the Fifth Avenue and 72nd Street property, sold to make way for a 12 story apartment building. The league spent months looking for a new location (ironic for having a real estate man in their midst) and finally found space for a diamond at West End Avenue and 95th Street. The newspaper described the lot's recently excavated mounds of earth, like grated nutmeg and frozen solid, resembling the earthworks trenches on the front lines of the war. As before, the middle-aged men played baseball in freezing weather. Some of the hardier and reckless individuals dared pneumonia in shirtsleeves and flannels.

For the first time in his life, John got unfavorable press when the newspaper described his less than stellar performance as a pitcher. "Kid de Saulles, known to Yale men as a football player, was the star moundsman for just one inning. In that time the Calumet Club was winning its victory. De Saulles may be a great backfield player, but as a pitcher he doesn't figure. Every one of the opposing bats-men took delight in banging the ball to every corner of the lot and Kid de Saulles retired, the rest of his team mates urging him to send in his resignation. In reality he pitched the second inning and this was the one fraught with disaster, for he didn't get a man out and when the session was ended... nine runs had been scored."[102] Approaching 38 years old, he started to recognize that he was losing his youthful edge.

In the spring of 1916, John sent word to Blanca in Chile. He implored her to come back to the United States and bring his son little Jack home. A big bouquet of flowers—perhaps his trademark gardenias—came delivered with the telegram. Whatever he wrote, it reached into her heart and moved her to tears, because she responded.

Blanca journeyed back to the U.S. with three-year-old Jack by way of Jamaica. Her steamship was now able to go through the newly constructed Panama Canal instead of the treacherous long route around Cape Horn or the arduous overland railroad. They arrived in New York on April 13, 1916 a few days after Blanca's 22nd birthday celebrated at sea. When her steamship *Almirante* pulled into Ellis Island, and she saw John standing on the pier, her "heart sank" at the sight of him[103] because he looked so ragged. After only a year apart, he had seemed to have aged a decade.

At that time, John shared a residence in Manhattan with his brother Charles. They lived like bachelors in an apartment at No. 4 West 57th Street, the Duke of Manchester's former haunt. Charles de Saulles was also married but like John worked in the city apart from his family and sent money back home to support his wife and two young children. According to Blanca's testimony, John arranged for his wife to stay in another residence at 10 East 60th Street. Surprised and insulted, she suggested that his brother move away and they could be together, but John refused. Blanca said she had no choice but to accept the arrangement.

On Easter morning, 10 days after their arrival, John borrowed his son for the afternoon. Blanca stayed behind at her apartment, alone, and soon received a delivery of flowers with a note attached: *To our one and only sweetheart, from Big and Little*

Jack. She waited several hours, and when her two gentlemen returned, John told her of what great fun they had enjoyed at the Bronx zoo. Nearly forty years old, he acted fourteen when he poked at the caged lions with his stylish walking cane. The great cats' roars sometimes frightened the little boy and sometimes sent him into fits of laughter. In that moment, it seemed like a good day. After John said his good-byes, little Jack blabbed to his mother the rest of the story. "Miss Jo is a lady who was with us. Daddy called her Jo and told me to call her Miss Jo and not to tell you anything about her."[104]

This anecdote was told later at Blanca's murder trial to illustrate for the jury what a scoundrel John de Saulles had been. Imagine the gall, to bring his mistress Joan Sawyer on a trip to the zoo with his innocent little son as a witness! Yet we only have Blanca's version of this story. The four-year-old never gave a deposition or appeared in court; all of the child's quotes were hearsay taken as fact. We'll never know why she stayed home alone... why she did not join in a family outing to the zoo together with her husband and her son. Perhaps she was battling one of her mood swings in the chronic depression that plagued her. On that bright, sunny Easter morning, in spite of how desperately she wanted to be happy, she was no fun to be around.

At the murder trial, the prosecutor read another letter from John de Saulles, written to Blanca in 1916 to inform her that he had purchased a new house for them in the exclusive suburbs on Long Island. This rare, candid note from John supported what the in-laws were saying, that Blanca shared some responsibility for the disintegration of their marriage. "For the last four years you have refused to live with me as my wife. You have shown me no consideration whatever, and have been disrespectful and rude. In no way have you been playing the game for my sake, that's sure. If you won't play it for Jack's, I don't know what will appeal to you. In entering the new house I am getting for you, you must turn over a new leaf." [105]

જ•ન્ઙ

The future silent film star Rudolph Valentino arrived at New York's Ellis Island in December 1913 as an 18-year old Rudolpho Guglielmi. He came alone to America seeking a bright future along with thousands of other Italian immigrants. Unable to speak much English, he struggled at odd menial jobs, often homeless and sleeping on benches in Central Park, until he got his lucky break as a waiter in a high class restaurant. From there, he discovered that he had a natural grace and a talent for dancing. As feminism was gaining steam, rich lonely women enjoyed more independence by paying handsome young men to ballroom dance with them.

Blanca de Saulles was one of those lonely New York socialites who enjoyed his "taxi dancing" services as a way of coping with her older husband's long absences. Valentino later admitted to a gossip columnist that Blanca had taken his breath away. "For years I had cherished a picture in my mind of how the perfect woman would look, a picture composed of the things I had read and some of the great paintings I had seen. When Mrs. de Saulles stood before me it was as though the picture had come to life. I adored her. She seemed so far above me that I never dreamed she would look at a mere tango dancer."[106]

Later, at Blanca's murder trial, the prosecutor tried to shake her story of being desperately unhappy in the marriage. They quoted her personal letters that she had written to John, "...in which she said she had danced her 'heels off,' and was asked how she reconciled it with the statement that she was depressed and suffering at that time, she answered: 'We don't dance with our hearts.'"[107]

Blanca Divorced John

Love is not two people looking at each other
but two people looking ahead in the same direction.

ANTOINE DE SAINT-EXUPÉRY
POET AND AUTHOR

On July 28, 1916, Blanca filed a lawsuit to end her marriage with John de Saulles. Her representative was the Manhattan law firm of Prince & Nathan that, until now, had specialized in lawsuits, bankruptcies, property disputes, and insurance fraud. John's lawyer was Lyttleton Fox, a fellow Yale alumni and Phi Delta Phi fraternity brother,[108] whose experience also involved real estate and financial matters. In years to come, Lyttleton Fox would gain fame as the attorney settling the contested estate of Jay Gould the millionaire. Family Law was not yet considered a specialty field.

In the divorce proceedings held in early August 1916, Blanca appeared to be a saintly woman neglected by her playboy husband. The messy details were described in open court, of John's wild parties with showgirls from Broadway's Ziegfield Follies, of behaving like a bachelor in his New York apartment when his faithful wife and innocent baby waited at home. His friendship with President Wilson, his heroics on the varsity football team at Yale, his successful business dealings... all of it seemed to mean nothing.

133

The original court records from any divorce action are sealed until the 100-year mark, but Valentino's biographer Emily Leider was able to examine the papers after filing a motion to temporarily unseal them for research.[109] Witnesses testified under oath about John de Saulles's shameless philandering with Joan Sawyer, the popular ballroom dancer. John's personal valet Julius Hadamek had seen Sawyer spend the night in his employer's bedroom and found her hairpins on the pillow. Sawyer's cook Anne Curtis had seen them kissing on several occasions.

Fig. 22 - Joan Sawyer

Sawyer's professional dance partner Rodolpho Guglielmi (Valentino) also testified in divorce court. He told of attending a dinner party where he observed Joan Sawyer calling him "Jack" and "sweetheart." Valentino had traveled as a dance partner with Sawyer to Washington D.C. to perform for President Woodrow Wilson, and another time they had performed at a theater in Providence, Rhode Island. He described John de Saulles and Joan Sawyer sharing a hotel room, coming and going in taxicabs at indiscreet hours, or traveling together. "Mr. de Saulles and Miss Sawyer shared a drawing room on the train. I had an upper berth in the same car, opposite their drawing room."[110] From these intimate quarters, he claims that he saw birth control paraphernalia in Sawyer's luggage. Of all the witnesses, Valentino's testimony is the most extensive and detailed.

Fig. 23 - Rudolph Valentino, silent film star

At the murder trial a year later, transcripts of the divorce hearing were entered as evidence of her miserable married life. Excerpts were quoted in the newspapers. Valentino's motives for testifying against his partner had been questioned at the time, but not too deeply. He was still just a ballroom dancer and not yet a famous silent film star.

> *Lyttleton Fox, lawyer for de Saulles, asked Guglielmo [sic] in cross-examination if he did not consider that he was doing an ill turn to his theatrical friend in giving his testimony.*
>
> *"No, I don't think so," replied Guglielmo.*
>
> *"Are your relations friendly with Miss Sawyer?"*
>
> *"They were friendly the last time I saw her; I don't know, now. I volunteered to testify here."*
>
> *"For what reason?"*
>
> *"I have a special reason, but if you don't mind I won't go over the matter," replied Guglielmo. He was not pressed on this point.* [111]

Why did Valentino throw his dance partner under the proverbial bus? The most obvious answer is unrequited love, because Blanca de Saulles asked him for a favor. Leider's biography speculates that Valentino saw himself as a knight in shining armor rescuing a damsel in distress. He felt a deep kinship with Blanca being from a Latin country. He had never experienced the bigotry of white Anglo-Saxons until he came to New York and learned new words for himself, like *dago* and *wop*. Here was a lovely young Latina married to an all-American man of the type that he clashed with as a slick-haired, tuxedo wearing tango dancer. He and Blanca were almost the same age, two youths alone in a foreign country. She was literally a Madonna with an infant son being screwed over by a self-entitled, much older blue-eyed playboy.

This is the scenario portrayed in the newspapers of the time, and after a hundred years, it is generally accepted at face value. To this day, in Valentino's biographies and internet websites, John de Saulles is remembered as the first of many celebrities, politicians, and sports stars who cannot control their sexual urges. We expect rich and powerful charismatic men to behave badly since the days of *droit du seigneur* enjoyed by feudal lords of medieval France.

While doing research into the history of New York's divorce laws, I began to look at the de Saulles divorce saga from an entirely new perspective.

Adultery proved in court was the only way to end a marriage in New York at that time. Unlike today, with the modern concept of no-fault divorce, it was legally impossible in any state in the U.S. to end a marriage simply because both parties wanted out. Other states allowed for such things as desertion and cruelty, but New York was very slow to catch up. Little by little, they added abandonment and abuse to the list but until recently couples in New York still had to file a lawsuit and prove wrongdoing with evidence and witnesses. It wasn't until August 2010 that Governor David Paterson finally signed the state's first no-fault divorce law. Supporters hail the milestone, saying it will end the long on-going practice of "institutionalized perjury" in divorce courts and finally bring New York's family law into the 21st century.

John and Blanca's 15-year age difference, the clash of North and South American cultures, her clinical depression, or a general disappointment with each other were simply not enough reason to legally end the marriage.

In reality, most so-called divorce lawsuits in New York were performance pieces. A wife would tell a fictional story of abuse, neglect, and cheating. The husband would make little or no defense. Lawyers winked and played along. Judges accepted manufactured evidence and rubber-stamped divorce decrees. A secret cottage industry of fake adulterers sprang up in New York, and some women made a living at pretending to be a husband's mistress in staged photographs. In the 1930s an article appeared in the *New York Mirror* titled, "I was the Unknown Blonde in 100 New York Divorces," telling the story of Dorothy Jarvis a fake mistress for hire.

It's not clear how far back in history this unavoidable fraud goes. For all I know, John de Saulles may have invented the idea.

John obviously wanted out of the marriage as much as Blanca did. He could have elected to divorce her by traveling to Mexico, or Reno, or France, as those places had more lenient laws. Among his inner circle, Paris was the go-to place where marriages would be dissolved for his cousin Philip Lydig (1919), his cousin Maurice Heckscher (1927, first wife), and even Rudolph Valentino (1925). Marriages ended without complications in Reno, Nevada for his friend Judge Edward P. Coyne (1910) and later his cousin Maurice (1933, second wife). Clearly, John did not have an aversion to traveling, as he had journeyed all the way to Paris to marry Blanca in the first place. With a degree in law from Yale, he had to be clever enough to know that, by hosting in his home stadium, a rough skirmish lay ahead; but then, quarterback John de Saulles always had a good game plan.

By going through the New York Supreme Court, he actually had more control over the process and the outcome. His fraternity brother Lyttleton Fox represented him in court, whereas in France or Nevada he might have to rely on strangers for counsel. Although it was Blanca who technically filed the lawsuit, John probably instructed her in what to do. The mistake in looking back at the incident with modern eyes is that we assume a woman is taking charge when she files divorce papers against her husband.

139

Looking again through the mind of a lady in 1916, a different scenario emerges. Divorce was a sin in the church, and it is hard to believe that she would initiate the process without being coaxed into it. Blanca's most natural impulse would be simply to return home to Chile and stay with her mother indefinitely, as she did before. John as a salesman might have offered her true freedom with an attractive deal that he later reneged upon. As she said at the murder trial, "When we discussed divorce, he promised to give me the baby, but he broke his word."[112]

What if the divorce hearing was all a charade played for the courts? What if this was Valentino's first scripted performance and he had been coached in what to say, either by Blanca, or perhaps even by John de Saulles himself?

The de Saulles hearing fits the pattern of divorce court theater perfectly. For a graduate of Yale Law school, and with a top-notch lawyer on the case, he put up a suspiciously pathetic defense. That is, he put up no defense at all. The list of so-called witnesses for the plaintiff were: 1) an employee of the woman he was supposedly having an affair with, 2) the woman's dancing partner, and 3) his own personal valet. Either they are committing acts of betrayal against their employers or they are committing perjury at the request of their employers. Joan Sawyer's cook faded into obscurity, Rudolpho Guglielmi moved to Hollywood and became an actor, so the only witness left to examine is John's valet Julius Hadamek.

Considering the almost feudal culture of New York's high society at the time, it is hard to believe that Julius Hadamek would disclose such intimate secrets even to a court of law. A butler's primary duty was to cover-up illicit visits and destroy evidence of love affairs. More telling is the fact that Julius Hadamek kept his job after supposedly dragging his master's name through the mud. He was on duty faithfully serving at John's home on August 3, 1917 the night of the shooting. At various times through the years, Julius worked for both John and his brother Charles, and John would specially request his services on that fateful day. This shows that, in years to come, despite the damning testimony at the divorce hearing, Julius continued to be a valued employee.

Also entered into evidence were Blanca's personal letters mailed to her traveling husband over the years. The letters (quoted earlier) are indeed sentimental and portray a young wife abandoned by a husband off pursuing his fortunes. A great deal of weight is given to this stack of letters, both at the divorce hearing and at Blanca's murder trial, but neither court asked the most important question. Where did these letters come from? She would not have used carbon paper to copy personal correspondence. Yet the tear-smudged pages that she had mailed away reappeared in her hands. The letters had to come from John's own collection, which

141

means he selected which ones to provide and which ones to conveniently misplace.

Far from being blind-sided by Blanca's filing an action of divorce, John de Saulles appears to be the quarterback with a great deal of control over the game played out in the courtroom. Also, coming from a family of career politicians, Blanca would understand how to be flexible with facts in order to accomplish one's goal. If the divorce hearing was scripted by John de Saulles like a Broadway play, then Blanca was a willing co-star. To gain their freedom by proving adultery, there was really only one logical choice for who would play the part of the cheater. Men could get away with a soiled reputation; women could not. John de Saulles took one for the team, let himself be tackled as the adulterer, and scored a winning touchdown.

The court proceedings wrapped up quickly in early August 1916, and the question of alimony and counsel fee was settled by stipulation. As the "loser" of the "case," John paid Blanca's $1,000 attorney fees.[113]

Blanca chose to take a personal holiday in Europe after the divorce hearing and before the courts settled the matter. On August 27, 1916, she sailed off to Europe[114] with her sister Amalia and brother Billy, leaving her son little Jack behind in the U.S. in the care of his nanny "Booby" Anne Mooney. According to the newspaper, quoting her attorney Mr. Nathan, the interim court order granted Blanca full custody of the child but John had the right to visit for three-hour intervals at any time he desired. The order also granted John full custody for one month from September 15 to October 15. If the newspaper has accurately reported the terms, then the timing of Blanca's holiday is peculiar. She departed New York several weeks before she would be obligated to hand over little Jack to his father. She stayed in England past the date when she would have been entitled to have him back in her arms. Given the options of staying in the U.S. with her child, or embracing her family on foreign shores, Blanca chose to sail away.

Blanca, her sister Amalia, and brother Billy along with his wife and small daughter, departed Liverpool on October 25. The group with their entourage of servants returned to New York on November 3, 1916. Arriving on the same passenger list was a 27 year old French maid named Suzanne Monteau who would soon become Blanca's favorite servant. Miss Monteau would stand faithfully at her mistress's side on the night that John de Saulles was shot dead.

In December 1916, the referee of the court filed a recommendation to grant the divorce. Lawyers haggled behind closed doors over the terms of child custody and division of property. The court entered a final judgment on April 12, 1917.[115]

Blanca's victory at ending her marriage was bittersweet. The court did not award the mother full custody, as she had hoped, but divided the child between them. Here and not in the courtroom was where everything went wrong for her. At this point, she may have realized that she had been playing John's game; she had carried the ball following his play-by-play sketch only to discover herself scoring a touchdown for the other team. The terms[116] were that little Jack would spend a total of seven months with his mother and five months with his father, but staggered so that the little boy was bouncing back and forth every other month. The judgment forbade either of the parents from taking the child outside the United States until after the war when, someday, the oceans would be safe again. The sinking of the *Lusitania* was still fresh in everyone's mind, and since January 1917 the Germans had engaged in unlimited submarine warfare. The Kaiser's U-Boats torpedoed anything in the Atlantic Ocean. The terms also stated that, even when the seas someday were safe for travel, neither parent could take the boy to any other foreign country except England. Blanca's hopes of cutting herself free of this man, and taking her son home to Chile, were dashed to pieces.

The divorce settlement went into great detail about little Jack's future. John was required to pay a generous alimony of $300 per month. In the event that Blanca remarried, then he would pay half that amount ($150) for care of the child until little Jack reached the age of majority. At the time of starting school, the custody schedule would change so John would have the boy during the academic term and Blanca would have custody only for summer vacation. The visitation rights were flexible, if requested in writing by either party, but repeated the condition that neither parent could interfere with the boy's attendance at school by traveling. It clearly prohibits either parent from taking the boy to any other country except for England or the "United States of North America," meaning not South America... not now, not ever. Clearly the only things John de Saulles cared about were his son's education and preventing Blanca from taking him to Chile.

Blanca stated in her affidavit, annexed to the final divorce decree, that she had "faithfully lived up to her duties as a wife, having followed her husband to a strange land."[117] She also declared that she was being forced into a very painful position. "I must either give up my child and let him remain here or give up my mother and my friends in Chile."[118] She did not have a chance at getting a fair shake in the settlement. The legal system favored the paternal line and her attorney Mr. Alfred Nathan was no match for negotiating with alumni of Yale Law School. Her ex-husband gained complete control of little Jack's future; the boy's whole life was mapped out as a carbon copy of his father.

Valentino and the Vice Raid

To generalize on women is dangerous;
to specialize in them is infinitely worse.

RUDOLPH VALENTINO

About five weeks after the divorce hearing, Valentino was arrested in a vice raid near Carnegie Hall in the dark early hours of Tuesday, September 5, 1916. He was thrown in jail for several days and to earn his freedom he spilled his guts to the cops, giving up evidence of blackmail schemes and police corruption.[119] Biographer Emily Leider could not locate the police file although she did get her hands on the original indictments. The court charged both Rudolpho Guglielmi and a Mrs. Thym with operating a disorderly house, a term broadly defined in the state laws of the time as "...a place for the encouragement or practice by persons of lewdness, fornication, unlawful sexual intercourse, or for any other indecent or disorderly act or obscene purpose."[120] This could apply to anything from a full-out brothel to a private home where consenting adults enjoyed a good time.

Several of Valentino's biographies over the years have noted the incident and made connections to Blanca de Saulles's divorce hearing. Some have wondered if Joan Sawyer called the police because her name was slandered by her friend's betrayal. In her 2003 biography *Dark Lover*, Emily Leider proposes that John de Saulles had used his personal connections to arrange the

147

vice raid as retribution for the incriminating testimony "...of a mere tango dancer and an Italian immigrant to boot."[121] This latest theory is taken as fact by Valentino fans and circulates widely on the Internet, but actually, there is no evidence of John's involvement in the vice raid. Leider's speculation is based on a vague reference in the *New York Times* to a tip-off from a "well-to-do New York business man." Although the scenario is possible—John de Saulles had the means and opportunity to call the cops—it is more likely that he had nothing to do with it.

The vice raid happened five weeks after the divorce hearing, which seems like a long time for John to sit on his hands. He was an impetuous man of action who charged with the football through the opposing team's line; who hopped on a ship to sail around the globe when asked to help with the Woodrow Wilson election campaign; who jumped in his automobile and sped across town to bail an old friend out of jail; who pursued and married a girl because she smiled at him under the warm South American sun. If John had a "beef" with Valentino, he would not wait around five weeks stewing and scheming, but he would have confronted him on the spot. It's not that he couldn't have arranged the vice raid; I think it's just not his style.

Consider the possibility that the evidence and testimony were exaggerated, if not mostly fictionalized under John's theatrical direction, and he was pleased with the outcome. John got everything he wanted in the divorce settlement, so why would he be angry at all? He did not take retribution on his own valet Julius Hadamek for testifying. It seems odd that John would retaliate against a tango dancer but not discipline his own servant for violating his master's sacred trust.

John's primary concern was keeping custody of his namesake son. He had agents of the Dougherty Detective Agency trailing Blanca, during and after the divorce proceedings, to prevent her from skipping out of the country with the boy. John's instructions were, "...if the boy should ever be taken to Chile there would be no chance on earth that I could ever get him back again." [122] He might have hoped to catch her and Valentino together and accuse her of being an unfaithful wife, to get full custody of his son. John had played enough football that he knew how to win a game by sizing up his opponent's weaknesses. Valentino was notoriously poor at controlling his emotions and it was obvious to everyone in the divorce court that he adored her. John had everything to gain by letting Valentino walk around free with his big brown puppy eyes yearning for Blanca. Getting him thrown in jail makes no strategic sense.

Blanca had a stronger motive to erase Valentino from the scene. She had more than a reputation at stake if she was branded an unfit mother. Later, after Blanca shot her ex-husband, the newspapers hinted at gossip that John de Saulles, "...though found guilty of misconduct in the divorce suit, had been able to make favorable terms because he had threatened that he would bring a counter suit, naming a dancer often in company with Joan Sawyer..."[123] The judge deciding on guardianship of little Jack during the murder trial also remarked upon how strange it was that the mother was not granted full custody. "I do not quite understand why the Supreme Court originally saw fit to deprive the mother, being the innocent party to the divorce action, of the sole custody of her infant under fourteen, ordinarily granted to innocent parties. No doubt there were good reasons."[124] Leider's biography refers to another article in *Variety* magazine that gossiped about Blanca being seen in public with a professional dancer.

Blanca feared a scandal showing that she was not as innocent as she seemed. If Valentino was jailed for pimping, then Blanca could play the victim again if their relationship (whatever it was) ever came to light. Blanca did everything she could to distance herself from the Latin lover. A few weeks after the divorce hearing, she sailed to Europe with her sister Amalia and brother Billy, putting the whole Atlantic Ocean in between her and her faithful tango dancer. Her steamship arrived in the U.K. on September 3. If the vice raid on September 5 was a frame-up to get Valentino jailed, then it's more likely that Blanca could have arranged it. Her trip to Europe was a great alibi, and the timing is very close.

Silent film fans look back at this incident through the filter of his later fame and assume Valentino was the primary target of the police warrants. However, in 1916 he was not yet a movie star; he was just another ballroom tango dancer in tuxedo and tails. He lived two blocks away from Mrs. Thym in an apartment at 264 West 57th Street near Broadway and Columbus Circle. This neighborhood was known as the Tenderloin, one of the worst crime-ridden areas in the United States notorious for its nightclubs, gambling joints, and brothels. Either through naiveté or the influence of shady friends, the young Rodolpho Guglielmi was also capable of getting into trouble all by himself.

The house where the vice raid happened was the residence of Mrs. Georgia A. Thym[125] a middle-aged woman who had lived at 909 Seventh Avenue for a number of years. I have found her in public records as far back as 1905 listed as Gertrude E. Thym,[126] a single woman living with one female servant. Elusive and mercurial, almost nothing is known about her.

Mrs. Thym's humble brick flat house between 57th and 58th Streets was overshadowed by the magnificent luxury apartment tower known as Alwyn Court that, today, is on the National Register of Historic Places. Constructed between 1907 and 1909, Alwyn Court's façade is a glorious work of architecture in the French Renaissance style with dragon-style salamanders and gingerbread trimmings. Soaring 12 stories high, one can look over the whole green expanse of Central Park from the top penthouse. Alwyn Court's spacious suites would later be subdivided during the Depression into smaller apartments, but at this time it was occupied with globe-trotting bankers, lawyers, engineers, and their staff of maids and butlers. Mrs. Thym lived, literally, on the fringe of elite society.

Since the police file has gone lost (by accident or on purpose), all we have are the newspaper accounts of the vice raid. Compared to other mundane stories of corruption and politics, this one has some fairly entertaining details. With apologies to the late Mr. Valentino, here is the whole embarrassing story. It appeared on Wednesday, September 6, 1916 in the *New York Times,* "Vice Squad In Raid Near Carnegie Hall: Story of Narragansett Pier Witness Leads to Arrest of Cabaret Dancer and a Woman." A similar version was published the same day in the *New York Tribune,* "Dancing 'Count' Held In Vice Raid, Rodolpho Guglielmi Taken by Squad Headed by Swann's Assistant."

The District Attorney's office received a tip-off from an unnamed source identified in the *Times* only as a "well-to-do New York business man, who said that he had been victimized." Assistant District Attorney James E. Smith brought two detectives with him in the early morning hours of September 5 to raid the flat house at 909 Seventh Avenue. Smith told reporters that Mrs. Thym's place had been the site of countless "vicious parties" where social climbers became victims of blackmail after indiscreet visits there. The police had not interfered until now, a reference to rampant police corruption that the head District Attorney was working to clean up.

When plainclothes detectives first entered the apartment, the *Tribune* reports that Valentino tried to convince them that Mrs. Thym was out of town, and he threatened to call the police if they did not leave. Smith called him out by name, "Hello, Rodolph!" to which Valentino replied, "Rodolph hasn't been here since last May." The detectives were not fooled and hauled the both of them off to jail.

The *Times* identified Valentino as "a cabaret dancer, who said that he was a recent dancing partner of a woman well known on Broadway." The *Tribune* is less kind, referring to him as a "dancing count" and a "bogus marquis." The *Tribune* also quotes Smith's description, "He is a handsome fellow, about twenty years old, and wears corsets and a wrist watch. He was often seen dancing in well known hotels and tango parlors with Joan Sawyer and Bonnie Glass." Note how the newspapers slammed his masculine image (or lack thereof); he wears a corset under his trim-cut tuxedo; he has a dainty wristwatch at a time when "real men" carried only pocket watches; he dances the tango.

The newspapers make very little mention of the mysterious Mrs. Thym, the owner and resident of the house in question. They report only that she is gray-haired and about fifty years old. Leider describes the interior of her apartment as "decorated with heavy draperies and suggestive oil paintings"[127] and it was probably a brothel. Mrs. Thym may or may not be her real name. Her presence is completely upstaged by the antics of the Italian tango dancer requesting his one-and-only phone call.

Valentino chose to reach out to Frank Lord, Second Deputy Police Commissioner, of all people. According to the District Attorney, who seems to enjoy blabbing freely to the newspapers, Valentino said into the telephone, "I'm in bad trouble, Frank. I wish you would come down here and help me."

Reporters wasted no time in tracking down Deputy Commissioner Lord across town, and found him later that evening at the Prince George Hotel. According to the *Tribune*, Lord confirmed that that he knew "Rodolpho," but could not recall where he had first met him. Valentino had told the prosecutor that he had dined with Lord in the Domino Room of the Café L'Aiglon, in Philadelphia, when Joan Sawyer was with the commissioner. Lord denied to the reporters that he ever dined with him in

Philadelphia but admitted he had seen his dance performance. "This afternoon he called me on the telephone and said he was Rodolpho. I didn't know him until he finally said he was Miss Sawyer's dancing companion. Then I remembered who he was. I told him I was unable to help him."

Both Mrs. Thym and Rodolpho Guglielmi were arraigned in the Court of General Sessions and held in $10,000 bail each. They provided information about blackmail schemes and police corruption. Bail was soon reduced to $1,500 and, after producing the smaller sums, they were released.

As far as anyone knows, Valentino never saw Blanca after the divorce hearing and the humiliating vice raid. His partnership with Joan Sawyer broke up as exhibition dancing was losing popularity, being replaced with the dazzle of motion pictures. Joan Sawyer herself appeared in a 1917 silent film, *Love's Law*, but her career as a dancer and an actress drizzled away into obscurity. Valentino left New York City to join a traveling musical revue titled *The Masked Model* as a chorus line dancer. The show toured across the country and delivered him to California where he had hopes of getting into motion pictures too.

Three years later, after his first blockbuster movie "Four Horsemen of the Apocalypse" set him on the path to stardom, either the Hollywood studios or Valentino himself tried to wipe away the stain on his good name. A small article appeared in the

New York Tribune, May 20, 1920, "The Case of R. Guglielmi, How He Was Detained as a Witness Only and Soon Released," obviously written by attorneys. "Mr. Guglielmi was not taken into custody upon any criminal charges. The Tribune did not assert or intend to assert the contrary and it neither made nor intended to make any reflection upon him. He was detained only as an expected witness against others, and when it appeared that there was no charge and no evidence that he had committed any offense, he was speedily released from custody by order of the Supreme Court. Mr. Guglielmi, formerly a professional dancer, has recently entered the motion picture field."

Here is the end of Valentino's involvement with Blanca de Saulles. When she killed her ex-husband, he was 3,000 miles away struggling to get his first bit parts in Hollywood movies. No doubt he was deeply shocked and saddened by the sensational headlines in Los Angeles newspapers, yet he made no attempt to contact Blanca or offer support. He did not testify at her murder trial. For the rest of his tragically short life, he would dodge the questions of gossip columnists and answer as vaguely as possible when pressed to describe his relationship with Blanca de Saulles.

The Divorcée Life

Parting is all we know of heaven,
And all we need of hell.

EMILY DICKINSON
POET

President Woodrow Wilson appealed to Congress on April 2, 1917 to help make the world safe for democracy, and the United States declared war on Germany a few days later. Neutrality and pacifism ended as the country entered into its first role of intervention on foreign soil. Everyone's thoughts turned to events in Europe. Every young man enlisted, suited up, and shipped off. Rudolpho Guglielmi, in San Francisco working as a professional dancer, complied with mandatory registration with the U.S. draft board on June 1, 1917 and claimed exemption as a non-citizen.[128] The newspapers of the time are full of outrage that able-bodied immigrants, or alien slackers, were able to avoid service. As the film star Charlie Chaplin explained later, civilian clothes became the uniform of shame. Valentino also tried to register for Italy's armed forces (an ally of France) but he was rejected because of his poor eyesight. He desperately wanted to serve in the military and return to Europe where his widowed mother and his sister were suffering under the German occupation. Fate had other plans for him. The only time he would wear a soldier's uniform was in the movies.

Blanca de Saulles showed very little concern for the war in Europe. The only involvement of Chile was as a supplier of natural resources. The iron mines in Coquimbo once owned by her family now belonged to Bethlehem Steel, and Charles M. Schwab increased his already enormous fortune by supplying the war effort. The nitrate deposits mined in the north of Chile were in high demand as an ingredient of gunpowder. It seemed the ideal time for her to return to her homeland and reap the profits, to live high on the wave of Chile's prosperity. Yet she was chained to New York by the terms of the court's decree.

The divorce settled and entered its final judgment in April 1917, just one week after the U.S. entered the First World War. As young Americans donned uniforms and hopped aboard steamships to cross the Atlantic, the de Saulles's living arrangements turned to the suburbs. Blanca and John de Saulles lived within a few miles of each other in two separate homes on Long Island.

Once known as the birthplace of the poet Walt Whitman, and the summer White House of former president Teddy Roosevelt, after the turn of the century Long Island became the Shangri-La retreat of the rich and famous. The so-called Gold Coast is where F. Scott Fitzgerald was inspired to write the *Great Gatsby*, the dream land where wealthy built royal castles as vast miniature kingdoms, where adjectives like opulent, luxurious, and extravagant fall short of reality. These multi-million dollar estates did not have street addresses, they had names like celestial planets unto themselves: Meudon, Caumsett, and Falaise. The captains of industry who reaped the profits of the Industrial Revolution had a fantasy lifestyle constructed around indoor tennis courts with glass ceilings, stables for herds of polo ponies, packs of fox-hunting hounds, landscaped gardens with European sculptures and spacious ballrooms for hundreds of party guests. Among these elite of high society, the "norm" was crystal chandeliers, antique furnishings, walls and ceilings decorated with carvings and gold leaf. One fellow decorated his master bedroom with what he claimed was Emperor Napoleon's actual furniture. Others brought in sections of medieval castles, brick by brick, reassembled into towers facing the harbor. The eccentric lady of Ferguson Castle paved the floor of her main dining room with the tombstones of children's graves stolen from cemeteries in Europe. This was a brief era that, like the bubbles in the champagne fountains, sparkled brightly and vanished. In a few years would come the stock market crash of 1929, the Great Depression, and the burden of mounting taxes. Many of the extraordinary Gold Coast mansions have fallen to ruins, abandoned with boarded up windows, rumored to be haunted houses overgrown with vines and spiderwebs. More than half succumbed to the bulldozer to make way for middle class housing developments and expressways. A few of them, like Old Westbury

Gardens, are maintained as tourist attractions or private schools and museums.

Blanca's monthly alimony checks paid for a home called "The Crossways," located in the community of Roslyn, New York. It is a quiet village near the northern shore, nestled in a harbor that empties into Long Island Sound. The yachts and fishing boats, and the cries of sea birds, would almost feel like home on the bay at Viña del Mar. Yet it was almost worse for it to be similar, like the scent of a home-cooked meal that she could not taste. Blanca's homesickness intensified over the summer of 1917, along with her growing frustration of being like a caged lioness in the house that John provided.

John went into debt with mortgage on a country home known as "The Box," formerly owned by the bodacious Emily Ladenburg—a wealthy widow who galloped on cross-country fox hunts at the Meadow Brook country club alongside the men, and who shocked polite society by rejecting a side-saddle. The two-and-a-half story, Georgian style colonial manor house occupied eight acres[129] of secluded grassy woodlands, located off a curve in the Vanderbilt highway race course near the village community of Westbury. Compared to the extravagant castles of tycoons on the Gold Coast, his home was a relatively humble structure sized more like a Vanderbilt's guest cottage. A gravel driveway circled through a row of towering evergreen trees. An exterior of wood paneling, painted zinc white, offset a shingled roof. Dark window shutters framed the sliding windows. Two square brick chimneys poked up at either end.[130]

John spent his final days doing high profile real estate transactions as he had been doing for the last few years. He bought a horse for himself, and a matching pony for little Jack, and tried to play polo half as well as Maurice or his friend Louis Stoddard at the Meadow Brook country club. He engaged in Red Cross fundraisers for the war effort and, like the rest of the country, hoped to see victory for Allies very soon. A few days before his death, he wrote a letter to President Wilson's staff offering to organize another league to benefit the U.S. Navy.[131] He would not live long enough to make that happen, nor would he see the Armistice, the Treaty of Versailles, or the League of Nations. The whole world was on the verge of change, shaking off the crumbs of the 19th century, but John de Saulles would not be a part of it.

Fig. 24 - John L. de Saulles Jr. as an All-American cowboy

At home, John invested thousands of dollars on capital improvements to his home. Unlike any residence he had owned before, "The Box" had a playground with a chute slide and a seesaw constructed for his son's amusement. At nearly five years old, little Jack de Saulles Jr. was a rugged boy, robust and large for his age. John taught him to ride a scaled-down polo pony. There is a photograph of father and son, side by side in matching suits and horses.

Fig. 25 - John de Saulles and his son, on polo ponies

John had reached that age, drawing closer to the dreaded fourth decade when he was finally slowing down to reflect upon his life. He had "been there, done that" by traveling the world, always restless...always on the move. He had spent his life staying in apartments that were extensions of college fraternity houses or in five-star hotels as a vagabond on his way to somewhere else. He had been a visitor at Doña Blanca's home but did not have a room of his own in the Quinta Vergara palace. Until this point, he had never known the stability of a hearth and home. In every endeavor, in building an intercontinental railroad in South America or financing a grand hotel on the Long Beach boardwalk, he dashed onto the playing field, put in a good game, and retreated to the locker room.

At last, in the final months of his life, he started to put down roots. With a son to be responsible for, John de Saulles learned to look outside of his own hopes and desires. He had begun to peel away the blinding layers of charming narcissism that had guided him this far. He was on the verge of re-inventing himself, a self-centered Peter Pan transforming into an adult. No longer "Kid de Saulles," it appears he was trying to become a father.

Maurice Heckscher provided to the newspaper a carbon copy of a letter that John had written to Blanca dated June 30, 1917, about one month before she killed him. Maurice published the letter to counteract the public image of his cousin as the cold-hearted playboy and deadbeat dad that Blanca (speaking from her jail cell) made him out to be.

"My Dear Blanquita: As you know the Box is dedicated to little Jack. He has around him there all his pups, including his pony, dogs, &c. He seems to enjoy these attractions so much and they have kept him out of doors the whole day long. It appears to me rather hard on the little fellow during these hot days to move him to some place where he will not have the freedom of the country such as he is now having at Westbury. Therefore, merely as a suggestion to you that during this coming month of July, which period belongs to you, I will be perfectly willing to step out of the house and not return there until my period comes around again. I will further offer you my servants which would be, of course, at no cost or expense to you. Inasmuch as this property is solely for little Jack's use you need not consider me in the matter in any way, and at the same time I think that, with Jack's interest uppermost in your mind, you should put aside any little personal feelings that you might have and let the boy continue to enjoy the magnificent life that he has been leading and which has kept him in the pink of condition. Of course, this is all up to you. It is for you to decide, and should you care to take him away he will be ready at the time appointed by the court." [132]

If anything, the letter shows that John truly cared for the welfare and happiness of his little boy. He may have been an absent husband, but at this point, he was no absent father. In that summer of 1917, little Jack played catch with his father on the grassy lawn. He learned to wrap his tiny fingers around the lacings of a leather football, under the guiding hands of the famous Yale quarterback.

Blanca did not respond well to this letter from her ex-husband and she did not accept the offer. She retrieved little Jack to her Roslyn home "The Crossways" for the month of July. She felt deeply threatened that her son enjoyed time spent at his father's house, going to the zoo, riding in the automobile, playing with dogs and ponies. At home with Blanca and her timid French maid Suzanne Monteau, the active little boy simply did not have as much fun. I imagine she scolded him for running or shouting out loud in the house. Because of the divorce settlement, she could not take him home to visit her mother in the serene gardens of Quinta Vergara palace where no one ever ran up the stairs or shouted out loud. She felt trapped and alone, isolated from her family and her childhood friends. She lived near her ex-husband, but she was alone like a widow in her home. She was no longer Mrs. John L. de Saulles; she was a divorcée—a scandalous creature shunned by God and polite society. Now her most sacred role, that of mother, was slipping through her fingers.

Blanca watched with dread as her son transformed into a *norteamericano*. He spoke English, not Spanish, even with her. At the murder trial, she would accuse John and his relatives of manipulating the boy's affections against her, or that they instructed him to misbehave for her. The accusation seems far-fetched, a bit paranoid, clearly stemming from culture clash and innocent misunderstandings. Jack's sense of proper manners was being shaped in the United States into behavior that Blanca used to think refreshing and attractive. As a mother, not a teenaged girl, her attitude towards North American men had changed. Now, "confident" meant "arrogant", and "direct" meant "rude", and "happy" meant "foolish." When she looked ahead to the future, she did not see her son developing into a refined, dignified Latin gentleman like her older brother or her uncles, the sort of grandson that her mother Doña Blanca could admire. This image of manhood as a sensitive, soft-spoken fellow who treated women tenderly would be introduced to American culture by Valentino in later years, and his Latin lover style would impact Hollywood in the 1920s like a nuclear bomb. Physical weakness and emotional sensitivity were pounded out of young boys at an early age, then even more than now. Her *pequeño* Jackie was being groomed to develop into a Douglas Fairbanks type of "real man" full of athletic exuberance, but who would rather leap off a roof than bow to kiss a girl's hand.

More than learning the wrong kind of *machismo*, it pained her that little Jack was isolated from the heritage of his Chilean ancestors. He knew nothing of Blanca's paternal grandfather Maximiano Errázuriz Valdivieso at whose funeral 1,500 mourners wept in the streets of Panquehue. He knew nothing of Blanca's maternal grandfather José Francisco Vergara Echevers who built the town of Viña del Mar. The heroes of Blanca's heritage were unknown to her son, as little Jack was being taught to admire Abraham Lincoln not Federico Errázuriz Zañartu.

Also, she resented her country being taken over by North American business interests. Bethlehem Steel Corporation owned the Tofo Iron Mines that once belonged to her family, and other copper mines were owned by the American Smelting Company, Inc. where John's brother Charles de Saulles was on the board of directors. Charles M. Schwab, the Guggenheim copper tycoons, and the de Saulles family reaped profits off Chile's mineral resources especially now that the war in Europe was ramping up. Foreign investors, like ocean waves drawing away the sand grain by grain, eroded her country's value. She also mentioned these grievances at her murder trial, but the North American media found it easier to spotlight her motherhood instincts than to explore the complexity of international politics.

When her ex-husband and his North American relatives had control of her son, even for a few hours, she lost more than her child's companionship. She was losing a private war. The French battle cry, *"On ne passe pas!"* became Blanca's personal mantra as she hurtled toward her breaking point. The hurt and rage continued to build in her over the next few months, from April to July, as the weather in New York turned unbearably hot, steamy, and humid.

The night Blanca shot John de Saulles came at the end of a brutal heat wave.

The Night She Gunned Him Down

I shot him because he would not give me back my boy.

BLANCA DE SAULLES

A heat wave smothered the Northeast in the last days of July 1917. There was no relief from temperatures that stayed above the nineties for a full week. Air conditioners had not been invented yet, and blocks of ice were a luxury commodity delivered by horse and wagon. Humidity made the atmosphere into a steamy soup. Modesty prohibited men going shirtless in public, and women's layered dresses (with corsets underneath) covered them from chin to heels. Day and night, the people sweated and suffered and prayed for it to end. The New York Stock Exchange completely closed down. The Board of Health estimated that over 800 people perished in New York City alone, and almost 300 horses collapsed dead in the streets.

The heat wave finally ended on Thursday night, August 2, the day before Blanca killed John. In the afternoon, the thermometer reached 94 degrees—another day of a hellish inferno—until dark clouds gathered in the ceiling of the sky. A thunderstorm broke about 2:00 PM. Warm rain cascaded onto sizzling streets. Lightning jabbed close to the baked housetops but no one cared about the danger. Stormy winds driving the clouds also brought a genuine breath of coldness. Men and women leaned out from upstairs windows. The downpour splashed their sweaty

171

faces. Eyes closed with pleasure, they breathed clear air for the first time in a week. Lightning struck and killed a few people, burned out electrical connections to the suburbs of New Rochelle and Larchmont, and set a couple houses on fire. In a bizarre twist of nature, the rain in Westchester turned to hailstones the size of golf balls.

Friday morning, August 3, 1917, John de Saulles and the rest of New York awakened to weather that, if not refreshing, was a little closer to normal. Over breakfast he checked yesterday's baseball scores in the newspaper: the White Sox beat the Red Sox; St. Louis was shut out by Philadelphia; the Yankees were in third place in the American League standings. Front page headlines discussed the progress of the war in Europe with graphic tales and photographs of the Allies floundering in muddy trenches. News from Great Britain's political scene briefly mentioned an inexperienced young fellow named Winston Churchill.

John had lunch at Sherry's, an exclusive restaurant located across the street from Delmonico's at the corner of Fifth Avenue and 44th Street. He flashed his winning smile to the cordial owner Louis Sherry and said, "Put it on my tab." Joining him were his sister Caroline Degener and his friend Marshall Ward. His father Major Arthur de Saulles had come to visit from Pennsylvania and felt ill in the heat. John invited them all out to Long Island to "The

Box" for supper and to escape the brick-and-steel buildings that made the city feel like being inside a gigantic bread oven. In addition to his usual staff of house servants, John called on the services of Julius Hadamek. At various times over the last several years, Hadamek was employed as chauffeur and butler by either Charles or John, the brothers trading the loyal Austrian immigrant back and forth as needed.

Blanca did not endure humidity or extreme heat and felt sick most of the day. Her son had been in her custody throughout the previous month of July but he was due to be with his father for the upcoming month. A verbal revision to the schedule of divorce terms, a "gentleman's agreement," gave her the right to have little Jack a few more days at the beginning of August... or so she understood.

John de Saulles telephoned Blanca around mid-morning on Friday and requested his son. He explained that his father and sister were visiting and wanted to see him. Blanca assumed that he would keep little Jack only for the afternoon and return him promptly by 7:00 PM, a point later disputed by John's sister. Caroline Degener insisted that John understood the boy was rightfully to be under his roof for the entire month of August, and he had been generous in allowing her these few days. They did not put anything into writing; whatever they agreed, it was all done on the telephone.

Blanca's household servants later told reporters that, when she had consented to hand her son over to John, she was in a "reckless state of mind" and played with little Jack "in almost a hysterical state of animation."[133] Since the divorce she had become a recluse. She rarely entertained or hosted parties, had almost no visitors at "The Crossways" and spent most of her time fixated on her son. She never went dancing anymore. Story telling and reading to her son occupied their time, as Blanca had never engaged in sports like horseback riding, tennis, or golf. She did not share her son's love of polo ponies.

As the hour approached for little Jack to go to his father's house, Blanca first ordered a house maid to prepare the boy for the trip. Then she changed her mind and took control; she washed and dressed the boy herself.

A servant from John's house arrived in an automobile and asked for the boy. Blanca showed offense that the maid had presented herself at the front door instead of at the rear. She ordered the maid away and demanded that a "better mannered person" come to get the child. The maid accepted the lady's scolding on her breach of etiquette and departed without the boy. About half an hour later, the automobile returned with a manservant who knocked with proper humility at the back entrance.

Blanca stalled some more by hugging and kissing the child at the doorstep, but finally had to let him go.

Some time later, Blanca telephoned Constable Leonard Thorne at the local police station to report that marauders had attempted to enter her garage. The constable replied that he was not available that evening, but made an appointment for the following day to interview her about the burglary.

According to her house servants, Blanca ordered dinner about 7:00 PM but did not feel like eating. She paced around the house, anxiously expecting her boy to return. Restless, she became more agitated by the minute. Weather was still miserably hot, and thunder boomed overhead. A full moon shined like a white eye through rare breaks in the black clouds.

Over at the "The Box" John and his family had a pleasant supper. Little Jack was an exuberant child, boisterous and active, and remarkably articulate for a small boy. He delighted his grandfather. They talked and laughed, and after supper adjourned to the living room at the front of the house. Arthur de Saulles was not feeling well and lay down on the sofa to rest. John sat in an armchair near his father and, while reading, kept up conversation.

After supper, Marshall Ward loitered near the large fireplace but I doubt they had a fire going in this heat. He stared out the window at the looming storm and puffed on a cigar as men often did in the evenings. The newspapers described John's friend at the murder trial as a "little dapper man"[134] who walked briskly on his way to the witness stand. As a stock broker and financier, the soft-spoken Kentuckian was certainly no athlete; he was not on the interclub baseball team and did not play polo at the country club. Yet he was a familiar visitor at John's house, and little Jack knew him well enough to give him a nickname "the Wardie man."

Little Jack played with toys on the carpet and, from time to time, interrupted his father's reading with questions. They played music on a phonograph. Caroline as a dutiful aunt went upstairs and, with the help of house maids, prepared to put the boy to bed for the night.

Shortly before 8:00 PM, Blanca announced to her maid Suzanne Monteau that she was going to get the boy. First she called "The Box" and Julius Hadamek answered the telephone. When Blanca asked for her ex-husband, John instructed Julius to say that he had gone out to the country club for supper and would be away for about an hour. Julius repeated the white lie without hesitation. The question is whether or not she believed this feeble and obvious ploy to avoid her, and if she guessed from the valet's long pause... the whispering in the background... the change in his tone of voice... that John really was at home. Blanca told Julius over the phone, "I'll be right over and get Jackie."

Blanca called to Hamilton's Garage to order a taxicab. Mr. Raymond Hamilton, the owner, said that she phoned at least three times, each call more insistent than the last, demanding that a driver be provided at once.

Blanca then telephoned to David Stewart Iglehart who lived in Westbury not far from John's house. She knew Mr. Iglehart through his wife Aida, a Chilean elementary school classmate. Mr. Iglehart had traveled to South America a few years before John's railroad venture as president of an import business (W.R. Grace & Co.) and a steamship line. The Igleharts had returned to the United States recently with their seven-year-old son. On this night, Blanca reached out to Mr. Iglehart as a man who also lived a mixed marriage to a Latin woman. The mirror opposite of her marriage to John, the Igleharts' marriage was successful and not plagued with torment.

Mr. Iglehart testified at the trial, "She told me that she was very anxious about her boy, and that she was afraid that some accident might have happened to him, because he was kept so much over time. She said she had learned that the boy had been put to bed, and that the father would not return from the Meadow Brook Club until after 9 o'clock. She asked me to go with her to get the boy, but I said that it was too delicate a matter for me to intervene. I asked her to come over to dinner before she went, but she said she was in too much of a hurry, and had called a taxi, and would go right after the boy and bring him back."[135]

No one knows if Mr. Iglehart regretted turning her down, if he ever dwelt on that phone call in years to come. If only he had accompanied her and tried talking to John, man to man, on her behalf. If only she had not felt so alone, desperate, enraged, and powerless as she walked up to her ex-husband's front door with a loaded gun in her hand.

James Donner, the chauffeur from Hamilton's garage, arrived at "The Crossways" in a taxi. He picked up Blanca, her maid Suzanne, and little Jack's favorite white bulldog named Sandy. The route from Roslyn to Westbury is roughly five miles, but it took a little longer than usual. As a stranger to the unmarked gravel trails, the taxi driver had to ask directions of a passerby for the route to "The Box" through the woodland meadows. Butlers and maids, groundskeepers, polo horse wranglers, and personal chauffeurs simply knew the way; those who did not know how to navigate the unmarked roads had no business being there. All along the way, Blanca kept urging the driver to hurry.

She carried on her lap a .38 Smith & Wesson revolver, the same handgun that John had bought for her years ago. This particular weapon had a five-bullet chamber, not like a cowboy's six shooter, and she had it fully loaded. The taxi driver did not notice her holding the gun. Blanca said later than she carried it for self protection on the isolated country road. Her burglary report supported this claim.

When they approached closer to "The Box" a little after 8:30 PM, Blanca ordered the driver to park and wait in the car with the bulldog. She said, "I told the driver to stop some distance away because I did not want to be seen driving up. I wanted to take the baby away and not be seen. I walked across a space toward the house, but in front of the door I saw Mr. de Saulles's car. I was awfully surprised to see it there."

The hedges and a row of tall evergreen trees blocked Donner's view of the front porch. From where he sat in the parked car, smoking a cigarette, he could not witness what happened next.

Blanca and her maid Suzanne walked up the semi-circle gravel path toward the front door. She brought the revolver carried in her right hand, tucked hidden away in the folds of her loose skirt. Because of the hot weather she wore a light cotton dress of pure white. Approaching the house by moonlight, she looked like a vengeful ghost.

Just before reaching the front door, she ordered her maid to stop and wait in the yard. Mosquitoes swarmed in clouds but Suzanne obeyed her mistress. The timid maid stood there in the gravel driveway, close enough to observe from behind, but not close enough to be involved.

Blanca proceeded up the stairs of the porch alone.

Caroline Degener, coming downstairs, was the first person to see Blanca through the window entering the screen-enclosed porch. Another butler opened the front door and announced the ex-Mrs. de Saulles's arrival. No one was surprised; the telephone call with Julius Hadamek had alerted them. Caroline greeted her, "Good evening, Blanca."

"I want to see Jack," said Blanca, meaning her ex-husband.

Caroline walked ahead, leading the way to the parlor where John, his father, and the little boy were enjoying their visit. Julius Hadamek lingered in the hallway ready as always to do his master's bidding. Marshall Ward retreated at the sight of her, either to the mantelpiece or—as Suzanne testified—he started to go upstairs. The elderly Arthur de Saulles continued reclining on the sofa.

On first hearing his ex-wife's voice, John came out into the hallway to prevent her going any farther inside the house. He stood at the interior doorway, blocking her from entrance to the parlor or approaching the little boy. "Hello, Blanquita," he said.

By coincidence, at that moment the telephone rang and Julius Hadamek went to answer it. The valet's withdrawal left John and Blanca standing alone in the hallway, face to face. They stood at most five to eight feet away from each other. At this point, the witnesses were not paying attention except for Suzanne the maid standing outside fraught with nerves. The others had seen the couple argue before and assumed that another verbal confrontation was about to erupt. Like most people, they turned away and allowed the couple some measure of privacy to hash it out.

Caroline took little Jack by the hand and escorted him out of the room. She led him upstairs to get ready for bed. Since the divorce, he had learned to keep quiet at times like these. He obeyed his aunt—anything to get away from seeing his parents argue. He did not witness his mother shoot his father, and over the next few months, would be kept mercifully uninformed of what happened.

Blanca appeared serious but outwardly calm. She stood still. She fixed her stare on him and he stared right back at her. They were almost the same height, eye to eye. Witnesses disagree on exactly what words passed between them. Basically, she asked for her son to be returned. The conversation was short and, though tense, did not escalate into a shouting match. They debated, they disagreed, but their tempers did not flare. Blanca recalled[136] saying, "I think it is mean of you to keep the baby from me this way. I want him. I have come to take him away."

John leaned his shoulder against the door frame, with what Suzanne described as an attitude of appearing bored. Off-guard, at ease, he did not perceive her as a threat. He still felt confident, in control of the situation and their relationship, as he answered, "You cannot have him now."

Blanca said that his refusal stunned her. "I felt a dreadful pain in the head." At this moment she claims she blacked out; the last thing she remembered was looking into his pretty blue eyes.

She raised her .38 Smith & Wesson revolver out of the folds of her skirt. She had been holding it all this time, as she did not carry a purse and had no pockets. From about five feet away, she aimed at his chest.

John shouted, "No!"

Suzanne Monteau said, "He was looking right at her.... His eyes were terrible. He looked as if he would jump on her."

John instinctively raised his left arm to shield himself; in that split second, it was the wrong reaction. He behaved like a third baseman raising his mitt to catch the ball, keeping his right arm free for throwing "out" a runner sliding into home base. His old mantra from his football days proved to be his un-doing, that a quarterback "should never under any pretext run up to make a tackle."[137] His training was to step backwards and let his team block the on-rushing line backers, only this time, he stood alone.

Blanca banged off every round in the chamber of her five-shooter. Not wild and erratic, not blinking, she focused straight ahead just as he had taught her to do while practicing at the country club. One, two, three, four, five... She squeezed the trigger in rapid bursts. Every bullet hit the target. The impact caused him to rotate. Shells clattered to the hard wood floor. As she kept firing, he ended up with his back to her.

John staggered over the threshold of the main door and collapsed halfway onto the screened porch.

Julius Hadamek dropped the telephone and rushed into the scene. "Madame, what have you done?"

She asked, "Can you get me my boy, now?"

"No, Madame, I can't do it."

Blanca set the empty gun on a small table near the hat rack. Appearing calm and emotionless, she quietly sat down on a couch. She did not move or speak but just sat there watching John bleed.

The witnesses became blind to each other's presence. Marshall Ward and Julius Hadamek each testified that they alone rushed to John's side. Arthur de Saulles strained to rise from the couch and weakly staggered to his dying son.

At first, they were not sure how badly he was hurt. He never lost consciousness and was still able to talk. He asked if his son was safe. He told them to call the police. As an athlete he was used to taking hard knocks and endured his pain quietly; he lay still and did not move. Most of the blood gushed out of his arm. The autopsy showed that several rounds struck him in the left bicep and hand. One bullet shattered his wedding ring finger. The fatal shot (or shots) penetrated his torso from the back, about two inches to the left of his spine, tore through his kidneys and punctured an artery. It would take a full two hours for him to bleed to death.

Caroline placed the little boy in the care of a servant, upstairs, and was the first one in the family to confront Blanca sitting on the sofa. "Why did you do this?"

"It had to be done."

"What do you mean?"

"I had to have the child." After a pause, Blanca added, "I suppose you had better send for the police for me."

Arthur de Saulles tucked pillows under where John lay, to try and make him comfortable. He examined the injuries and, from his experience as a soldier in the Civil War, began to realize how badly John was hurt. After a few minutes, the group lifted him off the floor and carried him into the parlor to place him on the sofa.

The police responded to the phone call within half an hour. The local sheriff Phineas Seaman arrived with his deputy Constable Leonard Thorne. The sheriff saw John de Saulles on the sofa, packed with blood-soaked pillows, and asked, "Who shot him?"

The answer, "Mrs. de Saulles."

"Where is she?" the sheriff asked.

The witnesses fussing over John had completely forgotten about her. Without anyone noticing, Suzanne the maid, sobbing and trembling, had enough presence of mind to do her duty. She had slipped into the house and retrieved her mistress.

The sheriff searched outside and, around the other side of the house, found the custom-built playground. There was a wooden see-saw, a swing, and a "shoot-the-chutes" about six feet high with a slide ten feet long emptying onto on a mattress. Blanca and Suzanne had been sitting for a while on the see-saw, and then had walked away from the playground to a hedge of dwarf trees about 50 feet out from the house. The two were standing in plain sight for the sheriff to approach them.

"Are you Mrs. de Saulles?" asked the sheriff.

"I am. Are you an officer?" she replied.

Sheriff Seaman asked for the weapon, and Blanca told him where to find it on the hat shelf. Constable Thorne returned to the house and took custody of the .38 Smith & Wesson. He opened the chamber to confirm that every one of the five shells had been discharged.

The two police officers escorted Blanca to their automobile. On the way, she stopped to speak to her taxi cab driver who amazingly still waited by the car. She instructed him, "Take good care of the dog. Drive to Roslyn and see my maid Louise and she will pay you for the trip."

Instead of taking her straight to jail, they first drove her to the private home of Walter R. Jones, the Justice of the Peace, who lived close by. In trousers and shirt sleeves, enjoying a cigar after dinner and getting ready for bed, Mr. Jones politely interrogated Blanca. "Why did you shoot him?"

She answered, "I shot him because he would not give me back my boy. I hope he dies."

John was rushed to Nassau Hospital, but he had lost too much blood for the doctors to do anything but make him comfortable. He sank into unconsciousness. Arthur holding his son's hand felt the fingers go colder and colder. He stood by John's bedside as the last breath sighed out of him. The father, who once stood by his child's cradle and grinned with pride at having a third son, watched a nurse in a white uniform mark data on a clipboard. "Time of death, 10:20 PM." Nearly two hours had passed since he was shot.

The phone call from the hospital came to the Justice of the Peace as he was signing her arrest warrant for attempted murder. On the spot, he discarded the first one and wrote a new warrant for actual murder. "Madame," he said. "Your wish has been gratified. Your husband is dead."

She replied calmly, "I'm sorry," but did not shed a tear. Throughout that night, as she was taken to Mineola Jail and locked in a cell, she remained calm and cool. Suzanne was also locked up as a material witness and spent the night sobbing behind bars. The sheriff and others remarked upon Blanca's lack of emotion, her serenity and composure, as if she were a guest at a lawn party and not under arrest for murder. They had never seen anything like it.

Modern technology spread the story overnight. Newspapers from coast to coast erupted with sensational headlines in their Saturday morning editions:

JOHN L. DE SAULLES SLAIN IN HIS HOME BY FORMER WIFE
— New York Times (NY)

DE SAULLES, YALE STAR, KILLED BY DIVORCED WIFE —
New York Tribune (NY)

DE SAULLES SHOT BY DIVORCED WIFE –
Boston Daily Globe (MA)

HEIRESS' BABY LOOKED ON AS
SHE SHOT HER EX-HUSBAND —
Washington Times (D.C.)

GLAD I KILLED HIM, SAYS MRS. DE SAULLES —
Evening Ledger (PA)

FORMER ENVOY KILLED BY WIFE —
El Paso Herald (TX)

POLICE PROBING MURDER MYSTERY —
Ogden Standard (UT)

HEIRESS SHOOTS ATHLETE —
Tacoma Times (WA)

J.L. DE SAULLES IS KILLED BY DIVORCED WIFE —
San Francisco Chronicle (CA)

DIVORCEE SHOOTS FORMER DIPLOMAT —
San Jose Mercury News (CA)

FAMOUS BEAUTY KILLS HER DIVORCED HUSBAND —
Los Angeles Times (CA)

John de Saulles's body was laid out for viewing at Campbell's funeral parlor in the heart of New York City. It is the same mortuary where, nine years later, Valentino's corpse would be displayed under a heap of white roses. That busy street corner, on Broadway near 66th Street, would someday see a riot as thousands of hysterical fans swarmed for a last view of the great Latin Lover of the silver screen. On a future day in 1926, Valentino's loyal fans, in shock at his sudden passing from appendicitis and a perforated ulcer, would clog the streets in mass pandemonium. Ladies would swoon in the summer heat. The windows of Campbell's funeral parlor would be smashed. A hundred people would be injured in the crush. Police officers mounted on horses would struggle for hours to control the mob.

But on August 4, 1917, for murder victim John de Saulles, only a small squad of uniforms was called to control the curious.

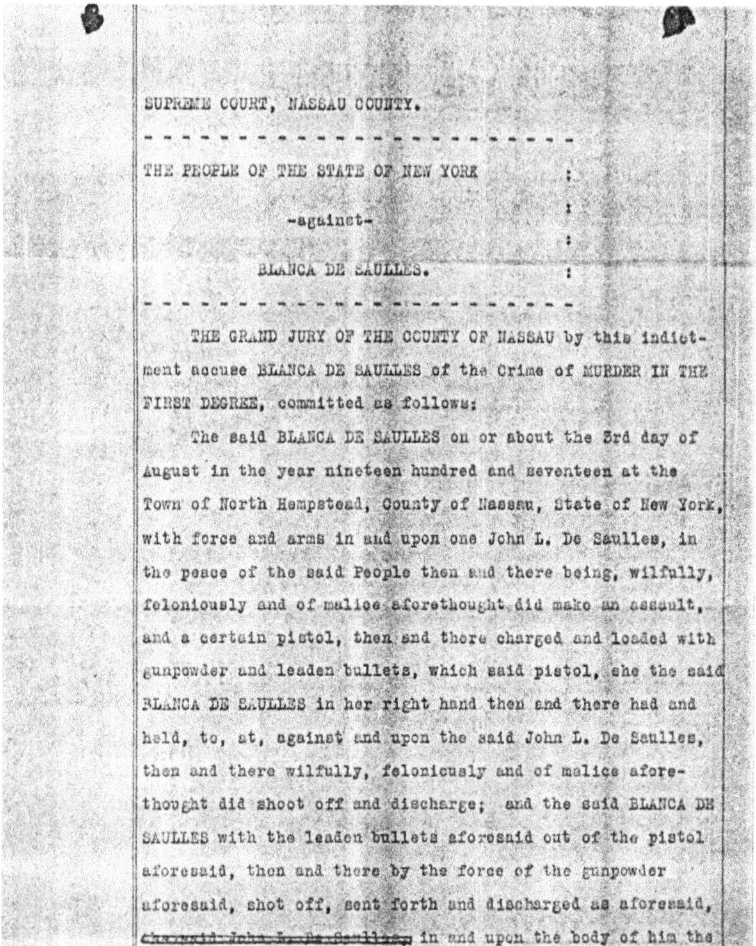

SUPREME COURT, NASSAU COUNTY.

- -

THE PEOPLE OF THE STATE OF NEW YORK   :

-against-   :

BLANCA DE SAULLES.   :

- -

THE GRAND JURY OF THE COUNTY OF NASSAU by this indictment accuse BLANCA DE SAULLES of the Crime of MURDER IN THE
FIRST DEGREE, committed as follows:

The said BLANCA DE SAULLES on or about the 3rd day of
August in the year nineteen hundred and seventeen at the
Town of North Hempstead, County of Nassau, State of New York,
with force and arms in and upon one John L. De Saulles, in
the peace of the said People then and there being, wilfully,
feloniously and of malice aforethought did make an assault,
and a certain pistol, then and there charged and loaded with
gunpowder and leaden bullets, which said pistol, she the said
BLANCA DE SAULLES in her right hand then and there had and
held, to, at, against and upon the said John L. De Saulles,
then and there wilfully, feloniously and of malice aforethought did shoot off and discharge; and the said BLANCA DE
SAULLES with the leaden bullets aforesaid out of the pistol
aforesaid, then and there by the force of the gunpowder
aforesaid, shot off, sent forth and discharged as aforesaid,
~~the said John L. De Saulles~~ in and upon the body of him the
said John L. De Saulles then and there wilfully, feloniously
and of malice aforethought, did strike, penetrate and wound,
giving unto him the said John L. De Saulles, then and there
with the leaden bullets aforesaid, so as aforesaid discharged,
sent forth and shot out of the pistol aforesaid, by the said
BLANCA DE SAULLES in and upon the body of him the said John
L. De Saulles one mortal wound of the breadth of one inch and
of the depth of six inches; of which said mortal wound he the

Fig. 26 - The criminal indictment

Preparing for Trial

I will throw away my license to practice law
if any jury which hears your story does not free you.

HENRY A. UTERHART
DEFENSE ATTORNEY

Blanca de Saulles started playing the media game right away by giving a sort of press conference from her jail cell, and in this strategic move she immediately gained the upper hand on her in-laws who were reeling from the shock. She publicly rehashed the tale of woe from the divorce trial and begged to see her little boy. In contrast to the famous murder trial of Lizzie Borden in the 1890s, there was no doubt that Blanca did the deed. The issue became *why* she shot him.

Her righteous justification and John's playboy character became the focal point of her defense. John became a villain who drove her to desperate measures, and John's family got branded in the role of cruel selfish people separating a mother and child. John's father made a brief comment through his lawyer defending his son's character. Maurice Heckscher made public the letter quoted earlier. Charles de Saulles issued a heart-felt statement to the papers defending his honorable name, but to no avail. The press lapped up the sensational headlines of a saintly woman wronged. What's more bizarre is that not only feminists (suffragists) but everyone fell under her spell: the all-male jailers, the all-male jury, and the stern no-nonsense judge joined in her fairy dance. In his closing arguments at the trial, the prosecutor would almost apologize for having to do his duty.

Reporters swarmed into the Long Island village to compete with each other for the scoop. They camped out with tents and folding cots on the grass. Newspapers in both English and Spanish covered the story, providing readers with juicy details of Blanca de Saulles's imprisonment at the Mineola town jail.

For her one-and-only telephone call, she reached out to John's cousin Captain Philip M. Lydig—the husband in another mixed culture marriage but one that was not holding together as well as the Igleharts.

Blanca telephoned the Ritz-Carlton hotel, where Captain Lydig was staying, and reportedly said, "Is that you, Captain? This is Mrs. de Saulles. I am in the Mineola County Jail.... I have just killed Jack. It was about the boy."

A few seconds later, Blanca loudly remarked, "Oh, I'm tired of hearing people say, 'My God.'" She slammed the earpiece onto the telephone's hook.

Later, the newspaper reporters tracked down Captain Lydig at the Ritz-Carlton and got this quote from him regarding Major Arthur de Saulles, "It was a terrible shock to my uncle, but he bore the blow like the old soldier that he is.... I cannot conceive any reason for the tragedy unless it be the act of a demented woman."[138]

Blanca's cold-hearted demeanor was observed by the Justice of the Peace who signed the arrest warrant, by Sheriff Seaman who brought her to the jail, and reported in the papers and remarked upon at her trial. She later claimed to have amnesia about this entire period of several days even while she outwardly appeared to be lucid and coherent, clearly understanding what she had done.

To reporters she articulated her lifetime of grievances against John de Saulles for squandering $47,000 of her inheritance and for selling $10,000 of her stocks without informing her. She accused him of scheming to marry her just for the money and that he was disappointed to discover after the wedding that the Vergara and Errázuriz family did not have as much capital as he thought. She also voiced a grudge against Bethlehem Steel Corporation for having ownership of and profiting from the Tofo Iron mines in northern Chile that had once belonged to her grandmother.

Fig. 27 - Nassau County Courthouse in Mineola, New York, circa 1917

Henry Ayres Uterhart, a renowned defense attorney, interviewed Blanca in the Nassau County jail on August 4. According to his later recollections, "It was impossible to get anything from her as she was still in a dazed bewildered condition and was unable to give any coherent answers."[139] He immediately sympathized with her, "a pitiful story of a poor little girl of 17, brought to a strange country, neglected, abandoned and betrayed, culminating in his brutal attempt to take away her child by force while he was still in her custody by Court decree."[140]

After the visit from her lawyer, her cool appearance cracked. Blanca fell into a state of nervous collapse, laying on her jail cell's cot, unable to eat, and calling out to see her son. Doctors

194

worried about her fragile health and feared she would have to be hospitalized. She behaved like the victim of a tragedy rather than the cause.

Because of her suffering from stress, Blanca was soon moved out of the jail cell into a spare room in Sheriff Seaman's own apartment. Not as strange as it sounds, the guest room had recently been used to hold another Long Island celebrity murderess accused of shooting her husband's mistress; Mrs. Florence Carman had been acquitted through the efforts of the same brilliant attorney. In fact, Blanca specifically requested the dream team of Uterhart & Graham as soon as she reached lock-up, leading some in the de Saulles family to speculate that she had pre-meditated John's murder so far as to plan for her defense in court.

The *New York Times* published a heart wrenching statement of John's father Major Arthur de Saulles. In the early days, the media had not yet chosen to make a martyr heroine of Blanca, and eagerly filled their pages with anything and everything related to the incident. "It is a matter of great grief to me that Mrs. de Saulles, having taken the life of my son, now chooses to heap calumnies upon him. Those calumnies will do no permanent harm, for the whole truth is certain to eventually come out. I know my son as he was and as few fathers can. Thank God, others know him as I did and hold his memory green and clean in their hearts. His faults he had in common with many other good men, but very few could justly claim to equal him in his splendor and his fineness. Jack was a man, every inch of him. I deeply resent the campaign of unjust attack that seems planned."[141]

Private funeral services were held at John's apartment on West 57th Street[142] with only close family and friends present. A spread of white roses covered the coffin along with a bouquet of pink rosebuds and a wreath of lilies of the valley. A quartet from Grace Episcopal Church sang a hymn. They buried him in the historic Green-wood Cemetery in the heart of Brooklyn.

The pall bearers included his cousins and friends Captain Philip Lydig, Maurice Heckscher, the attorney Lyttleton Fox, and Marshall Ward, as well as dignitaries William McCombs (President Wilson's campaign manager), "Big Bill" Edwards (New York city commissioner), Dudley Field Malone (former customs inspector at the port), and Rear Admiral Louis Gomez of the Chilean Navy.

John's father was said to have conducted himself with the stoic composure and dignity of an old soldier. His mother, a frail white haired old woman, broke down sobbing as the coffin was lowered into the grave. Here was a woman who had lost one child in infancy, another son at age 22, and now a third child was the victim of a shooting.

Charles de Saulles while traveling in the West first learned of his brother's death from the Saturday morning newspapers. He hopped aboard the midnight train from Colorado to be in New York as quickly as possible. He published a fierce statement defending his brother's name, explaining that the division of custody of little Jack had been modified since the divorce finalized, and it was mutually agreed that in July she would have the boy and John would have him in August.

> *"My brother not only did not misuse any of her private funds, but was most generous in his financial dealings with her, spending large sums to gratify her expensive tastes and to pay her debts.... My brother was a devoted and loving husband in their earlier days of their married life, and that it is the opinion of her friends, as well as of his, that the change in their marital relations was due to her conduct and her treatment of him.*

> *"I have it in writing over her own signature that their domestic differences were chiefly due to her own fault. It is certain that her friends continued to like and respect my brother after the divorce proceedings. I can mention no better illustration than the fact that the Ambassador from Chile, an old friend of Mrs. de Saulles and her family, had dinner with my brother only a few days before the tragedy.*

> *"Nor do I believe that her act was caused by an overpowering affection for the boy. She had agreed to a division of custody and even when she had him in her charge she did not spend all her time with him by any means. During the divorce proceedings*

she went abroad for several months, leaving the boy in this country. And the fact that she shot his father in the back, firing five shots in the presence of the little boy, my aged father, and my sister, seems to me to indicate that the welfare of the boy was not in her mind at the time. What more dreadful heritage could she have bequeathed him than that memory? The cold deliberation of her act; her statement immediately after the shooting: "Now send for a policeman," and her whole conduct seem to show a mind moved by cold fury and not by sudden anger." [143]

On August 10, little Jack was brought to the jail for a visit with his mother. The boy was in the care and temporary custody of Maurice and Louisa Heckscher. He was a happy, chubby little boy who hugged his mother and asked when she would come home. The family had agreed to act as John would have wished in showing Blanca every possible generosity. In other words, they let her see little Jack to quell her public complaints about how cruel they were keeping her son away from her loving arms.

The de Saulles and Heckschers had a real opportunity here to poison the boy's mind against her. No one had yet told the boy why his mother was locked up by the sheriff. He did not attend the funeral service. He kept asking, "Where's my daddy?" Luckily his aunt Caroline had snatched him out of the room just before the shots started, so little Jack was sheltered from the knowledge of what his mother had done. In this, they demonstrated that they had the boy's best interests at heart; they did not traumatize him for the sake of their own gratification.

Doña Blanca Vergara de Errázuriz supposedly declared, "I will not return to my country without my innocent daughter." Blanca's widowed mother boarded a steamship and vowed not to return home to Chile without her... at all costs. The unmarried sister Amalia came along on the same voyage. Doña Blanca wrote a letter to summon her son Guillermo, a diplomat stationed in Europe. To the mother's heart, nothing else in all the world mattered, and she asked him to drop his commitments to other countries and come to New York at once. The grand lady feared for her daughter's life, if convicted, and railed indignantly at the sensationalism in the American newspapers.

Billy Errázuriz left behind his pregnant wife Maria Edwards who was due to deliver their first and only child. He made a rendezvous with his mother in Havana, Cuba, then boarded the S.S. *Mascotte* which delivered them to Key West, Florida on September 7, 1917. From there, they traveled straight to New York. Billy was the foreign attaché to the Chilean legation in Washington D.C. and used his diplomatic connections to expedite their travels. They stayed at Blanca's home in Roslyn and made daily trips to the Mineola county jail to stand by her side. The delicate widow was not in the best of health and New York's heat and humidity sapped her strength. Doña Blanca would suffer several attacks of heart palpitations during the trial.

A representative of the Chilean embassy, Alberto Ried Silva, took the assignment to visit Blanca in jail and offer moral (if not legal) support. Officially, the embassy took a neutral position although the diplomatic staff privately rallied behind her. Ried described the experience in his 1956 memoirs, *El Mar Trajo Mi Sangre*. He first heard the news when the Consul General Mr. Carlos Castro Ruiz telephoned in the middle of the night: "Blanca Errázuriz just killed her husband John de Saulles. Be sure to come tomorrow, first thing, to my office."

Ried was overwhelmed with the media blitz, the neon banners flashing headlines in Times Square, the hundreds of newspaper reporters camped out by the jail, and reading about his own country in the American papers a thousand times. He recalled the almost universal support of the public, both in the press and among the people on the street. A merchant mariner handed Ried five gold coins as contribution to a nonexistent defense fund. A black shoeshine boy, learning that Ried was from Chile, polished his shoes free of charge.

In one remarkable incident, Ried brought a concert pianist Rosita Renard to visit Blanca in jail. The same age as Blanca, she was a prodigy who at age 14 made her debut with the Chilean

200

Symphony Orchestra. Miss Renard had come to New York to perform several solo concerts at Aeolian Hall that received glowing reviews. The *Times* described her playing as "a delight to hear, so spontaneous was it, so truly felt and assimilated, so crisp and sparkling in delivery, so delicately colored and so filled with a gracious and varied fancy."[144] Yet for all her talent, Miss Renard suffered from crippling stage fright that caused her to retire into a life of seclusion in Chile. She would not return to performing until the 1940s and appeared at Carnegie Hall in January 1949, the only time her talent was recorded before she died.

Blanca's "jail cell" (the sheriff's apartment) had a piano, and so Miss Renard gave an impromptu performance as if she were on stage at the finest concert hall. Prisoners in the jail yard, dressed in black-and-white striped coveralls, stopped their manual labors to listen to the masterfully rendered arpeggios of Beethoven, Chopin, and Debussy. For those few minutes, the hearts of brutal criminals softened a bit. They smiled tenderly at the musical poetry singing wordlessly from behind the barred windows.

Meanwhile, the wedding of John's niece Catherine McClintock turned into a dark and somber affair. She married Franklin Ellis, the son of Mrs. Gist Blair and a captain in the Army Corps of Engineers stationed at Camp Meade. Their wedding on November 7, 1917 at the Cathedral of St. Peter and St. Paul, in Washington D.C. had only relatives and friends present. Long months of her dreaming about this day show clearly in the bridal fashions. Catherine wore a luxurious gown of ivory satin, softened by chiffon and dotted in pearls, with a train that fanned out several feet behind her. A tulle veil flowed from a crown of delicate orange blossoms. Her four bridesmaids wore matching gowns of cornflower blue veiled in orchid tinted chiffon. In one brief afternoon, the happiest event of a girl's life quickly passed. No reception dinner was held. Yet their names shined in the society pages of that day. The newspaper took interest in mentioning that one of the wedding guests was Mrs. William Howard Taft, wife of the former president and a close personal friend of John's sister Armide McClintock. Catherine resumed wearing black—to mourn her murdered uncle—as she and Captain Ellis departed on their honeymoon trip.

In the months leading up to the trial, the de Saulles family petitioned for legal guardianship of John's son. The issue would be argued for a couple of months while the boy stayed in the temporary custody of Maurice and Louisa Heckscher. In the meantime, the family withheld the boy from visiting his mother in jail a second time. No matter how much Blanca fainted and cried out for her little boy, John's family would not divulge his whereabouts. They kept little Jack sheltered from his father's killer and from the newspaper reporters who madly knocked on doors trying to track him down.

Judge Fowler in deciding guardianship held to a general principle of giving preference to the father's side of the family. This means that although Blanca's relatives were available, staying at "The Crossways," they were not given any consideration. The judge's opinion went on to say that guardianship should rightly go to the uncle (Charles de Saulles) but "...he is not a fit and proper person, and that his ordinary residence has been the scene of debaucheries in times past."[145] Finally, on November 8, 1917, the judge appointed Maurice and Louisa Heckscher as custodians of the boy until Blanca's fate was decided.

The Nassau County grand jury indicted Blanca de Saulles for murder in the first degree on October 15, 1917. The District Attorney Charles R. Weeks requested the death penalty. If convicted, she would go to the electric chair.

The Trial

The crowds can boo as loud as they can cheer.

JOE DIMAGGIO TO MARILYN MONROE

Her trial began at the Mineola Courthouse on November 19, 1917 with jury selection. It took quite a few days to collect 12 middle-aged men whose opinions were not already formed by reading the newspapers. Women could not serve on a jury at this time, although the suffragettes gathered as spectators cheering for Blanca. She became a popular idol for a new generation of feminists who felt mistreated by a patriarchal society that favored the rights of men and fathers.

Editorials in the Chilean press saw Blanca as a genteel lady victimized by American greed. The author Manuel Ugarte in October 1917 outlined the litany of John de Saulles's abuses: rejecting her tender affections and deceiving her for material gain. He saw Blanca's violence against her ex-husband as striking a blow on behalf of all subjugated peoples. The *El Mercurio* newspaper, owned and operated by Agustin Edwards (the brother-in-law of Billy Errázuriz) would express relief after Blanca's acquittal, calling the tragedy a disgrace and not a crime, and heartily agreed with the verdict of forgiveness for this distinguished lady.[146]

A 1981 fire at the Nassau County courthouse destroyed most of the archives, and so the original transcripts of the trial are lost forever. All that remains are the newspaper accounts archived at the *New York Times* and the Library of Congress. Hordes of tabloid reporters scratched down every word in shorthand and rushed to typesetting for the great steel printing presses to crank out each morning's edition.

The Main Players

Judge: David F. Manning. This judge ran a tight ship, insisting on strict rules of decorum. On the first day, he issued his guidelines to the spectators elbowing and shoving each other in the hallway to try and get seats. The clerk of the court issued special admission passes to newspaper reporters and those with a legitimate reason to attend, such as attorneys and subpoenaed witnesses. The remainder of seats in the intimate little courtroom— about 175 chairs—was open to the general public on a first-come, first-served basis. Judge Manning especially prohibited eating lunch in court, taking photographs, and knitting.

Fig. 28 - Judge David Manning

Prosecutor: Nassau County District Attorney Charles R. Weeks. Recently promoted from his position as Assistant District Attorney where he had served for several years, he had a track record as an unrelenting and effective prosecutor. He strutted into the courtroom with statements of bravado like a boxer before a prize fight. His assessment of the crime was pre-meditated, cold-blooded murder, and he pursued that extreme position like a bulldog trying to bite the moon. Given the enormous public sympathy that had already built around Blanca in the media over the last two months, he might have fared better with plea-bargaining down to manslaughter. It appears that, with his promotion to District Attorney, he was eager to prove himself with a slam-dunk conviction.

Defense: Henry Ayres Uterhart. A man in his early 40s, a native of New York, he graduated Columbia University in the same year that Blanca was born. Although he now had a premier law office on Wall Street in New York City, his life had not been an easy one. When Uterhart was just three years old, his father died intestate (without a will) and he was raised by his widowed mother and grandmother. No doubt the family struggled and sacrificed to put him through college and law school. At the time of Blanca's trial, he was married and had one daughter aged 13 named Josephine. One has to wonder how deeply he was affected by his client's plight—a widowed mother with a small son to raise, and Blanca herself not much older than his own little girl.

Henry Uterhart's law partner of many years, Mr. John J. Graham, died from heart failure in late August while the firm was preparing for Blanca's trial. His obituary in the *New York Times*[147] reports that he had a nervous breakdown after defending the last sensational Long Island murder trial of Mrs. Florence Carman, and the strain had weakened his health.

Fig. 29 - Attorneys (left to right) John J. Graham, George M. Levy, and Henry Ayres Uterhart (circa 1914)

John Graham had a long career as a District Attorney and as a Surrogate Judge of Nassau County before going into private practice. The loss of his partner loss affected Mr. Uterhart deeply, but he did not withdraw from the case out of grief. He carried on and enlisted the help of another experienced lawyer.

In an ironic twist, the former Nassau County District Attorney Mr. Lewis J. Smith took a seat at the defense table. The man who had recently been the boss of Charles Weeks, the same man who prosecuted the Carman case, was now assisting Mr. Uterhart. This minor fact, mentioned briefly by reporters, deserves more attention than it received in the press. Mr. Smith gave the defense a huge advantage not only with his years of experience and judicial expertise, but because he knew the prosecutor Charles Weeks personally. He had worked with the man and considered him a good friend. He knew his habits, his weaknesses, his strategies. Uterhart did all the talking and the examination of witnesses, but behind the scenes Smith contributed a great deal to the preparation of the case. Throughout the trial, the defense was always one step ahead.

The 12 Men of the Jury. All of them were married men in their 50s or 60s, except one young fellow in his mid-30s. Every man had at least one child. They represented the average joe of the time who ascribed to traditional family values, who had old-fashioned ideas of women as delicate flowers to be protected. They came from a variety of social and economic backgrounds: farmers, grocers, a cigar manufacturer, a carriage trimmer, and a couple of real estate dealers. The jury foreman, John C. Bucken, worked as a bookkeeper for J.P. Morgan & Co. The juror Edward Pietech was an electrical engineer on the MacKay Estate—one of the spectacular Gold Coast mansions. Harry Livingston traveled frequently as an inspector for the railroad. Nicholas Schneider, age

37, was the village blacksmith who sometimes put horseshoes on the polo ponies at the Meadow Brook country club. In a composite photograph cut-and-pasted by the *Tacoma Times*, they appear to be a bunch of friendly uncles at a family picnic. The 12 men were given rooms at the nearby Garden City Hotel for the two week duration of the trial.

Fig. 30 - John C. Bruken (center) foreman of the jury

❧

Day 1, Monday November 19. Four men were selected for the jury, and dozens more potentials were turned away. In the laborious but necessary process known as *voir dire*, the prosecutor, the defense, and the judge interviewed each and every man randomly called from the general population. Mr. Uterhart rejected any man who had a son.

Blanca made her first appearance in court as a frail and dainty young girl. She wore a white blouse and a pleated black skirt. Her porcelain skin tone beautifully contrasted her dark eyes and neatly coiffed black hair. She exhibited good posture, with arms crossed on her lap like a lady, and for most of the day stared down at the floor so that her eyes appeared to be closed. Her gentle demeanor portrayed the exact opposite of the vicious, cold-hearted killer than the prosecutor was trying to prove her to be... beyond a shadow of a doubt.

Fig. 31 - Blanca de Saulles on trial for the murder of her ex-husband John L. de Saulles (1917)

❧

Day 2, Tuesday November 20. Blanca brought jury selection to a grinding halt, first thing upon entering court, with her "eyes flashing and lips trembling,"[148] agitated by the fact that her son had not come to visit her the day before. For the last several weeks, little Jack was brought to the jail on a regular schedule of Mondays and Thursdays. She conferred with her attorneys, and Mr. Uterhart on the spot began composing a writ of *habeus corpus* to compel the temporary guardians to bring the little boy to his mother. Judge Manning consulted in his chambers and ordered that the visits should resume on the regular twice-a-week schedule but that the boy should not be allowed in the courtroom. At no time would the boy be called to testify.

John's brother showed up in court dressed all in black for mourning. Charles de Saulles was determined to clear his brother's name and to see Blanca convicted. He brought with him several lawyers and private investigators that he had personally hired to assist with the prosecution. Surely the District Attorney did not appreciate the extra help, but he made no effort to order them back from peering over his shoulder.

Blanca's mother and siblings Billy and Amalia sat behind her in court. The Chilean consular officer Castro Ruiz helped escort the senior lady by the arm. Her family sat for hours with stoic composure under the scrutiny of newspaper reporters. They hardly moved and showed no emotional reaction to the sometimes grim questions asked of potential jurors. What are your attitudes on the death penalty? Are you willing to punish a woman as readily as a man? Finally, Doña Blanca felt overcome with heart palpitations and quietly withdrew to another room in the building to rest.

Four jurors were selected this day, bringing the total to eight.

҂ѻҩ

Day 3, Wednesday November 21. The court adjourned early in the day, at 2:00 PM, because only 10 jurors had been selected out of the pool of 150 men. They had reached the end of the list. Judge Manning ordered more residents of Nassau County to be called.

Little Jack was brought to visit Blanca in jail that afternoon. As he arrived, he ran the gauntlet of paparazzi. The flashbulbs of reporters' cameras exploded brightness. The boy held up his arm over his face and dashed for the door. He called out proudly, "They didn't get my picture because I turned my face away!"[149] During the visit, he sketched animals and airplanes with crayons. Blanca entertained him with stories of *Jack and the Beanstalk* and *Little Red Riding Hood*. This lovely domestic scene recorded in the newspapers charmed the readers and gave Blanca the image of a normal mother who adored her child. They might as well be sitting in their living room instead of jail.

The most noticeable details are overlooked by the Anglo-centric press. The boy speaks English, not Spanish, with his own mother. She tells him European folktales instead of Chilean ones. For the watchful eyes of the reporters, she put up a brave face, but behind the secret doors of her mind the resentment continued to fester. Her son had brown eyes and olive skin, but in his heart he was an all-American boy.

ॐ

Day 4, Thursday November 22. The last two seats in the jury box were filled in the morning, and the prosecution began with an opening statement.

Charles R. Weeks outlined their marriage from the Paris wedding in 1911, the birth of John de Saulles Jr. on Christmas Day 1912, the divorce hearing in the summer of 1916, and the granting of the final decree. He stated that the boy rightfully belonged in his father's custody for the month of August and did not address the statements made by Uterhart before trial that a verbal agreement existed between John and Blanca allowing her to have the boy until August 7. He related in detail the events of the shooting, from Blanca's phone call to Julius the valet, her summoning a taxi cab, walking up to the door alone, having a short conversation with John and then shooting him at point blank range. He wove the tale like a master story-teller, explaining how Blanca calmly greeted the police, how she instructed the taxi driver to take Sandy the bulldog home and get paid, and when she said, "I hope he dies," to the Justice of the Peace signing her arrest warrant.

Weeks said, "Her acts show that she understood clearly everything that was to be done, that she thought of herself and of others. She thought of lawyers, of her maids, of money, of the chauffer, and of everything in connection with her act. The grand jury has called this deliberate and premeditated murder..."[150]

The prosecutor then called his first witnesses. County surveyor George Fairfield showed his sketches of "The Box" and the surrounding geography. Mr. W.H. Pickering had enlarged photographs of the interior and exterior of the house. The owner of Hamilton's garage that furnished Blanca with the taxicab, and James Donner the chauffeur, described her trip from Roslyn to Westbury.

The most difficult testimony for the victim's family to hear was from Dr. Harry Warner who had conducted the autopsy. He used a laboratory assistant standing in the middle of the courtroom to point out where the bullets had struck. John's wounds took on significance as the prosecution wanted to prove that Blanca had shot him in the back, while the defense insisted that after Blanca started shooting he had tried to run away. This cowboy code of honor (shooting a man in the back) versus an implied insult to John's manly courage (being able to look death in the eye) distracted everyone from the more important fact. Whether or not John looked her in the eye or turned away is irrelevant; Blanca shot an unarmed man who had not threatened her.

Julius Hadamek, the valet, stepped up to the witness stand. He told the story again for what he hoped was the last time. Police interviews, a sworn deposition, and a grand jury hearing had forced him to relive that awful moment again and again.

On the night of the shooting, Julius had answered Blanca's telephone call. She first asked for "Jack," the nickname by which her ex-husband was known to his friends. John de Saulles standing nearby instructed his valet to tell Blanca that he was not at home.

"It was a lie, wasn't it?" the prosecutor asked.

"Yes, Sir."

"And you told it because he was your master and told you to tell it, isn't that right?"

"Yes, Sir."

Weeks should have stopped there. He was trying to establish reasonable doubt that perhaps Blanca saw through the valet's white lie. The District Attorney speculated that Blanca sensed her ex-husband's presence and knew very well that John was at home before she drove over there with her loaded gun. He failed to pursue his theory. He did not ask Julius how well he knew Blanca or if there were other occasions when Julius had lied at his master's command. He did not ask how much time passed in between Blanca's question and Julius's answer... a hand over the receiver... background whispers of what-should-I-say-to-her-Sir... tell-her-I'm-not-here...

Weeks asked if Mrs. de Saulles had said anything more. Julius replied, "She said: 'Don't say anything about my calling up. I'll be right over and get Jackie.'"[151]

This last statement thrilled the defense attorneys even though Julius was summoned by the prosecution. It supported their argument that Blanca had hoped to avoid her ex-husband at the time she drove over to the house. Indeed, the jurors later said that this testimony helped bring them to the conclusion that the shooting was not premeditated. Defense would claim that Blanca only went there to retrieve her boy, thinking that John was away at the country club, and she carried a gun for self-protection because it was a dark and isolated road. The prosecutor failed to ask the more critical question: why did she carry a loaded gun up to the front door of the house? If she had brought the revolver for self defense, then she should have left it behind in the taxi cab. She had arrived safely at her destination. She could see the family through the front window. If her intention was to retrieve her son, did she mean to pick him up in one arm with a loaded .38 in the other hand?

Blanca later testified that she saw John's automobile in the driveway, but the prosecutor also dropped that ball. He failed to point out for the jury that despite what Julius told her on the phone, she knew very well that her ex-husband was home at the moment she disembarked the taxi. Regardless of whatever her intentions might have been on the drive from Roslyn to Westbury, her mood absolutely turned murderous in walking those last fifty feet.

ॐ

Day 5, Friday November 23. Marshall Ward testified for the prosecution and, like Julius, described in detail what happened on the night that Blanca shot John. He said that he was in a far corner of the room and, though he tried, was unable to rush to the rescue before Blanca had discharged all five rounds. He related a touching scene of kneeling at his best friend's side.

Uterhart in cross-examination attacked Marshall's personal character. He mentioned the lawsuit in 1912 against the Paul J. Rainey Co., of which John de Saulles was then the president, and insinuated that both Ward and de Saulles were cohorts in a swindle related to the sale of those mortgage bonds. Blanca was not a victim of the alleged swindle, and it had no bearing on the case, but the judge allowed this evidence anyway. Uterhart also exposed Marshall's previous arrest for "fighting while intoxicated and using

219

indecent language in a Broadway café" for which he paid a fine.[152] Since it was not established if he was drunk on the night of the shooting, one would think his character flaws should not be relevant. Regardless of whether he hung out in bars and swore like a sailor, he saw what he saw. Quickly it was becoming a trial of credibility versus slander, of the virtuous and the decadent. Uterhart seized control of the trial's course and the prosecutor Mr. Weeks, time and again, scrambled to catch up to him.

"She shot my poor boy to death!" Arthur de Saulles testified at the murder trial in a deep voice cracked by emotion. He gazed straight ahead ignoring the demure young woman, his former daughter-in-law, who sat next to her attorney. Wrinkles sagged at the corners of his haunted eyes. His pale hand gripped the railing of the witness stand. Cold sunlight seeped through a gray window screened with purple vines. A single electric light shined over the judge's bench while dim shadows shrouded the rest of the courtroom. Behind the prosecutor's bench sat mourners of the victim, and Blanca's supporters aligned with the defense, but every other seat was packed with curious spectators hoping for a good dramatic show. Rain poured steadily and filled every pause with a whispering hush.

Once more, the elderly man shuddered to describe the night when his cherished son John Longer de Saulles had died in his arms after being shot at point blank range by his ex-wife Blanca. She had arrived by taxi at John's upscale Long Island home and demanded to take custody of her son. At that time, the four-year-old boy was upstairs with his Aunt Caroline being put to bed. John de Saulles coolly but firmly told his ex-wife, "No, you can't have him."

On the witness stand, Arthur paused. His blue eyes glazed over with the memory from three months before. He spoke in a quavering voice as if in a dream. "She said, 'If I can't have him, take this,' and then she fired three or four shots. My poor boy staggered and fell."[153] At 77 years old, and not in the best of health, he made a pitiable image of an old man grieving for his son. Uterhart did not cross-examine. After testifying, the Major staggered and Charles and Caroline rushed to his support. They took him by the arm and helped him totter into an adjoining room where he lay down.

Caroline Degener testified about greeting Blanca at the door, then going upstairs to put little Jack to bed. She had come downstairs just after the shooting and described Blanca's shocking attitude of calmly sitting on the sofa to watch her ex-husband bleed on the floor. "It had to be done," Blanca was quoted as saying.

Sheriff Seaman and his deputy Constable Thorne each testified about Blanca's conduct during the arrest and her matter-of-fact attitude. Justice of the Peace Walter R. Jones agreed with the officers, "Her calmness was surprising to me."[154]

The prosecution tried to make an issue of the murder weapon's mechanics and brought in an expert witness Captain William Jones of the local police department. The officer made a show of demonstrating that two motions were necessary to fire the revolver: the pulling of the trigger and gripping the safety clutch on the back of the handle.[155] This testimony was intended to show that Blanca had a clear presence of mind to pause in between firing each of the five shots and cock the gun with both hands. Again, they portrayed her as a cold-hearted gunslinger from the Wild West even as she sat quietly dressed in fluffy white blouses.

The handgun used in the crime was identified vaguely in the newspapers as a .38 caliber Smith & Wesson revolver. It was not a "six-shooter" but only held five bullets. Several five-shot models, in both single action and double action, were available at the turn of the century. A single action handgun requires the user to manually cock the hammer before firing each shot. For example, in cowboy movies, the gunfighter's technique is to use the left hand to "fan" the hammer for more rapid shooting. By the 1890s, single shot revolvers declined in popularity. The public showed a preference for double action revolvers, that is, where pulling only the trigger accomplishes cocking the hammer, rotating the cylinder, and firing a round. Double action or "self-cocking" revolvers outsold all single action guns from the First World War onward.

My best guess is that Blanca used the Hammerless Safety Revolver, a sleek and stylish design that encased the hammer entirely within the frame of the gun. This double-action model, manufactured as early as the mid-1880s, featured a spring-loaded safety plan and an inertia firing pin. The safety revolver went through a few models to fix persistent bugs in the barrel latching system. The fourth version of this model, produced around the turn of the century, featured a knurled-head barrel latch and was the most reliable, best selling variation of the pattern. Its design is quite different from a policeman's standard issue firearm, which explains Captain Jones's somewhat muddled testimony.

The defense a few days later destroyed the officer's testimony with their own expert witness: Blanca's sister Amalia. The newspapers remarked upon Amalia sharing her sister's exotic beauty, and the *Tacoma Times* described her "potent quality of attractiveness"[156] along with her stylish wardrobe. The smiling Amalia wore a navy blue suit dress and a dainty velvet hat for the occasion. She testified that women in Chile frequently carried revolvers for self protection and that she owned a gun herself. She handled the murder weapon expertly, without a qualm, and contradicted the police officer's expert testimony. She said: "You don't have to use two motions. Pulling the trigger presses the safety catch against the hand, and that is all that is necessary to fire it."[157]

Weeks did not produce another expert witness to refute the defendant's sister who clearly was not impartial or objective. He let the facts stand, that Blanca had quickly squeezed off all five shots in the heat of the moment. As he quietly sat down in his chair, he already knew that he had lost. He had failed to prove beyond a shadow of a doubt that Blanca had planned in advance to shoot her husband in gunslinger style.

Prosecution rested its case and surrendered the stage to Uterhart to make opening statements for the defense.

◈◈◈

Henry A. Uterhart was a powerful orator who immediately brought tears to the eyes of the jurors. He intended to prove that Blanca's temporary loss of reason had a number of underlying causes both emotional and physiological. He had declared before trial that he would not use alienists (an early term for psychiatrist) but would rely on medical testimony. Blanca had suffered from sunstrokes in the extreme summer weather, two previous head injuries had cracked her skull, and she suffered from anemia and a hypothyroid condition. Expert witness testimony would come later, so for most of his opening statement, Uterhart chronicled Blanca's miserable marriage.

He gave the jury a sympathetic version of Blanca's tragic life, how her father had died when she was only three, and how she was an innocent naïve child of 16 when John de Saulles aggressively pursued marrying her. He dramatized what a neglectful husband John had been with his drinking at cabarets and addiction to stage beauties. He told of how unhappy Blanca had felt as a vulnerable young wife alone in a foreign country, and how she had suppressed her misery and concealed her sorrows from John's family.

Blanca's sentimental letters became the heart of the defense strategy, but at first Uterhart had a problem discovering the documents. He told the jury, "Practically every letter she wrote to her husband was destroyed at the time of the divorce, and her letters to her nurse and confidante are the only instances we have been able to find where she expressed a single complaint to any one. If you ever heard letters that poured from a breaking heart, you will hear them when you hear these."[158] Yet, the letters from Blanca to John miraculously appeared a few days later. I can only assume they obtained court transcripts of the divorce hearing.

Blanca's defense attorney resurrected the divorce proceedings to demonstrate the long history of wrongs that she claims to have suffered. The woeful tale of John's infidelities with Broadway dancers, especially Joan Sawyer, became gospel truth and dramatized for its effect on the long-suffering wife. Blanca came out looking like a saint, and any suggestion that she had acted inappropriately by dancing the tango with a handsome Italian gigolo was never mentioned. This was the key to Blanca's defense: that the cheating son-of-a-bitch deserved what he got.

——

Day 6, Monday November 26 // Day 7, Tuesday November 27. Blanca de Saulles took the witness stand for two full days in her own defense, a risky move but one that Uterhart gambled on to win the jury's sympathy. She behaved like a demure schoolgirl, modest, subdued, and answering the questions posed to her. She spoke gently, charming the spectators with her slight lisp of Spanish accent mixed with a British intonation. She referred to her husband only by his surname and her accent made it sound like, "the soulless."

She was articulate and emotionally composed as she gave her account of that night. Blanca claimed she could not remember anything beyond the point when John said, "You cannot have him now or ever." She had no recollection of shooting him, speaking to the police, or how she came to be in jail. Because of amnesia, she could not testify about the shooting itself. Her mind was a complete blank as she pulled the trigger. As for the hours leading up to the shooting, she could only say that she had carried the gun for self-defense and that her sole intention was to retrieve her son.

"Then he looked at me and he said, 'You cannot have him.. You can never have him.' And I think I was stunned then, because I felt a frightful pain in my head. I still seem to hear those words." As her attorney later recalled, "She was seated in the witness chair with her back toward the window which faced to the west. It was about 4:30 in the afternoon of a late November day and the sun was just setting. As she said these last words, a bright ray of sunlight shone through the window and illuminated her head as if with a halo. The whole courtroom gasped. It seemed almost like a sign from Heaven that she was forgiven."[159]

The rest of the time, prompted by her lawyer's questions, she rehashed her long years of misery and neglect that drove her to desperation. Most of Blanca's two-day testimony focused on her unhappy married life by reading aloud from numerous letters (quoted earlier) that she had apparently written to John over the years.

Uterhart was careful to emphasize the passive tenderness of her hurt feelings, rather than allow any suggestion of resentment and long-festering rage that might indicate a mood inclined toward premeditated homicide. Yet to our modern sensibilities, outside the prudish Victorian mores of 1917, John's many offenses can hardly be called abusive. His faults were that he spent too much time on business and left his young wife in the care of family and servants. He socialized among glamorous silent film stars and English lords.

He dabbled in frivolous affairs with Broadway beauties. When he had visitations with little Jack, he treated the boy permissively with candy and took him to the barroom of the Waldorf-Astoria hotel. Blanca harped on her paranoia that John's family and servants—especially the Irish nursemaid "Booby"—were trying to manipulate her son's affections away from her. She claimed that they told little Jack he did not belong with her and instructed him to be naughty. Yet she never accused him of raising a hand to her, nor did he prevent her from traveling the world or dancing at parties.

Again, the prosecution floundered. He tried but failed to make the point that Blanca's grievances were not enough to justify murder. Weeks tip-toed through a cross-examination and even then was criticized for being harsh. He produced other letters that she had written to John that described her enjoying a grand time in London without him, going to shows and casinos, and socializing with men like Harold Fowler. It's not clear where these letters came from, certainly not the divorce transcripts. Perhaps Charles de Saulles had discovered them among his brother's personal things. Weeks confronted her about the affectionate tone of the letters, how she addressed them to John as "darling" and signed them "dada girl," but Blanca replied that she had falsely been sweet-talking John in her writing. "I thought the best way to keep a husband was to flatter him to death."[160]

No one mentioned if any of John's letters written to his wife had been saved. In the six years they had known each other, John had sent dozens of telegrams and an unknown number of love notes. Blanca's letters often mention replying to his correspondence, but she produced none at her trial. It appears the long suffering wife may have burned the whole stack after the divorce.

The harder Weeks tried to force Blanca into admitting that she had not been a proper wife, the more eloquently she denied it. She smoothly countered his accusation of dancing her heels off with the quotable line, "We don't dance with our hearts."

"Is it true that since the birth of your child you were a wife to your husband in name only?" Weeks demanded.

"That is not true," she said. "I was a wife to him, but I told Mrs. Heckscher, his sister, [sic] that I was not. That matter was my affair."[161]

The prosecutor kept probing to try and shake her claims of amnesia. Yet he failed to rattle her ladylike composure. She kept her hands folded in her lap and paused before answering each question. When a juror yawned, Blanca showed some spunk in her response.

"You are very tiresome in your cross-examination. I don't wonder the jurors are tired," she said.

"Oh, do I bore you?" asked Weeks.

"Oh no," Blanca answered. "I realize you have to do it."[162]

Blanca earned public admiration for her endurance under the grueling examination. She won the sympathy of everyone who heard the tale of her miserable marriage. The *Washington Times* headline declares, "De Saulles Widow is Unshaken in Story: Prosecution Fails to Shatter Testimony - More Tragedy Bared as She Tells How She Danced With Breaking Heart." The newspapers recorded her every blink, every sigh, every debutante blush. Handkerchiefs sopped up the tears flowing in the courtroom. Only the de Saulles family sat there with incredulous expressions to hear themselves described as cruel and manipulative.

An editorial, "Telltale Grey Hairs Testify of Suffering," appeared in the *Tacoma Times* evening issue, November 26, 1917. This is the best example of how the media portrayed Blanca as a victim and public opinion damned John de Saulles. Written by Idah M'Glone Gibson, the article describes "a beautiful Madonna face that a modern artist would give years of his life to paint." It compares her apparent grief at enduring a trial to the Virgin Mary "when she followed her Son up to the place of crucifixion," and observes that in her face "shines dimly the light of a sorrowing soul that cannot be quenched." The writer looked for a wedding ring and saw none.

> *"The light from the window came and rested on her wavy brown hair and there just at the temple I saw five white hairs. As I caught a view of them Blanca de Saulles put up her hand as tho' she, too, had perhaps discovered them for the first time this morning and she was still wondering what special grief had put them here. And I wondered if when she saw them she told herself as she fingered them: 'This one is for the long weary months when I was awaiting the coming of little John, when I had lost my girlishness and had become ugly and my husband left me for other gayer and more beautiful women. This one came from hurt pride. This one was for that awful time when my world had crumbled and disintegrated before my eyes and the only thing that seemed mine was my baby, and they took him from me, too. This gleaming white hair is the sad answer to my longing—my sleepless nights and lonely days without my boy. And this one has bleached with my tears as all these long months I have been alone incarcerated in a cell with only my despairing thoughts for my company.' Ah, what telltales those gray hairs among the beautiful brown tresses of Blanca de Saulles were!"*

❧❦

Day 8, Wednesday November 28. The defense had finished the previous day with the testimony of Ethel O'Neill, the nursemaid who had served Blanca just after little Jack's birth. She is the one to whom Blanca wrote so many letters complaining of her unhappiness at the in-laws' home in Pennsylvania. From this

231

witness came more tear-jerking anecdotes of John's neglect, of Blanca waiting at the train station and he never arrived, and of Blanca weeping over her son's cradle, "Oh, Toodles, daddy doesn't love us anymore!" Mrs. O'Neill mentioned a time that John received in the mail an autographed picture from a famous actress—the name withheld—and how Blanca had erupted in righteous jealousy.

On this Wednesday before Thanksgiving, the timid maid Suzanne Monteau took the witness stand. Once again, she described watching the scene from outside the house, the "awful dreadful" angry gleam in John's eye. She insisted that he had raised his arm in a threatening gesture just before she shot him. The prosecutor's cross-examination reduced the girl to sobbing.

Amalia Errázuriz testified about the childhood rough-housing that resulted in Blanca's first head injury, and the automobile accident in 1915 that caused a second crack in her skull. Amalia also described a conversation between John and Blanca just after their marriage, when John asked for management of the entire Errázuriz and Vergara family estate. Amalia said that "he became very ugly when this was refused him."[163]

D. Stewart Iglehart testified about receiving Blanca's phone call that asked him to accompany her to "The Box" and why he refused. "I said it was too delicate a matter for me to intervene."

Uterhart also called back some of the witnesses who had testified for the prosecution and under cross-examination pointed out inconsistencies in their stories. Marshall Ward insisted that he was nearby and witnessed every detail, but Julius did not recall seeing him in the room. Little understood back then, eyewitness testimony to a violent crime is extremely unreliable; if five people saw it happen, there can be five different versions.

Several physicians and alienists dazzled the jury with cutting edge science and psycho-babble. Expert witnesses displayed X-ray images of her previous head injuries: the childhood fall and the 1915 car crash. The prosecution, in rebuttal, called their own expert witness who interpreted the hole in her skull as an incomplete seal of the fontanel (the soft spot from babyhood) and not a fracture. Too little, too late, the defense moved past talking about the cracks in her skull and focused on her blood chemistry.

Medical doctors reported that she suffered from a hypothyroid condition that could affect a person's brain, eventually causing insanity and even death. They explained that Blanca was anemic and that this affected her mental capacity. Dr. Smith Ely Jeliffe testified about hypothyroidism causing amnesia and, "he did not think she knew who her husband was at the very moment of shooting and that she did not understand who he was afterward."[164] Dr. J. Sherman Wight compared her temporary amnesia to sleep walking or shell shock similar to soldiers on the front lines of World War I who were still able "...to understand and obey orders mechanically, though totally unconscious of what they were doing."[165] Dr. Wight finished with his opinion that it was unlikely Blanca would relapse into violence because she was receiving medical treatment in jail. In other words, as long as she kept taking her thyroid medication, she would no longer be a danger to society.

ॐ

Thanksgiving Day, November 29, 1917. Blanca de Saulles was permitted to host a holiday party for her fifty or so fellow prisoners at the Nassau County jail. The dinner of roast turkey, fruit, ice cream and soft drinks was served to a mixed group of murderers and arsonists and habitual drunkards. Her sister Amalia supervised the cooking and helped serve the meal. They had a jolly time and toasted success to a favorable outcome at Blanca's trial. One of the prisoners, a bartender, composed a polite note of which Emily Post would be proud. "Dear Madam: We desire to thank you sincerely for your kindness and thoughtfulness toward us today. It is impossible to put into words our kindly thoughts toward you. However, it is our earnest wish and desire that your next Thanksgiving will be spent with your darling family and your noble little boy." [166]

Little Jack was escorted to and from the jail by Harry V. Dougherty, the president of the Dougherty Detective Agency. John's family insisted that he—and not a subordinate detective— have personal charge of the boy out of fear that Blanca's relatives would kidnap him. Mr. Dougherty told reporters, "I have been watching the boy now for more than a year.... We had operatives constantly watching the boy while he was with his mother in the city and at her home in Westbury." [167]

The boy visited privately with his mother in the jail's upstairs apartment that served as her guest quarters. He dictated a letter to Santa Claus, which she wrote for him, asking for toy horses and a stable. Little Jack was still ignorant of the situation. He had been told that the jail was a hospital and his mother was confined there because of a sickness. This had satisfied his curiosity for a while, but he cleverly observed that chickens pecked about the jailhouse yard. Chickens did not belong at a hospital. Someone at the jail gave him a sheriff's badge to wear. "He went to one of the windows opening on the courtyard and called until he had attracted the attention of a few prisoners. Then he pointed at his badge and shouted: 'I'm the sheriff.'"

Henry Uterhart and Lewis J. Smith spent their Thanksgiving Day at the Garden City Hotel (where the jurors were also staying) to prepare for Friday's session in court. Uterhart composed a 20,000-word hypothetical question summarizing the defense's theory and soliciting an opinion from the alienists.

The prosecutor Charles Weeks told reporters that he decided to withdraw two of his expert witnesses. He feared that Blanca's charm had created an unconscious bias in her favor that tainted their testimony.

⊰∽⊱

Day 9, Friday November 30. The prosecution cross-examined the defense's expert witnesses, Dr. Wight and Dr. Jeliffe, about the X-ray images of Blanca's skull. The jurors almost fell asleep in their chairs during the reading of the hypothetical question now reduced to a mere 15,000 words.

This was the prosecutor's last chance to coax out of the expert witnesses the answers he wanted to hear. He tried pressing Dr. Jeliffe to agree that Blanca was not mentally unbalanced and fully realized what she had done. He cited previous testimony that she had requested someone to call the police immediately after the shooting.

"Would you still say that she did not know her act was wrong?" Weeks asked.

"I would want to know all the facts surrounding the statement," Dr. Jeliffe said.

After double-checking the transcripts for Suzanne Monteau's exact words, Dr. Jeliffe gave his opinion: although Blanca had asked for the police, it did not indicate she had a conscious knowledge of what she had done.

"What do you mean by 'conscious knowledge'?" Weeks asked.

"A knowledge clearly in her consciousness, with a complete realization of surrounding circumstances." [168] The doctor continued with his opinion, because Julius had first mentioned calling the police, that Blanca—in a vulnerable and confused state of mind—had merely repeated the valet's suggestion. Weeks could not rattle the doctor's analysis, and the diagnosis of temporary insanity was confirmed.

Aside from reporting on Blanca's wardrobe every day, the newspapers also captured her demeanor in court. She maintained a calm sense of poise throughout, hardly ever showing emotion even when on the witness stand. On the last day of expert testimony, they described her appearance and behavior as more alert than before. "Mrs. de Saulles was very pale, and from lines about her forehead and mouth appeared to be suffering as the long hypothetical question was being read. Later, however, when the alienists began to testify, she seemed to be very much interested in what they had to say about her. She gave more attention to the recitation of her symptoms than she had to any other testimony about the trial. She did something else yesterday which was new with her and might have indicated a growing consciousness of the serious position she was in. She would occasionally glance at the jury, as if to see how bits of testimony struck them. Her large black eyes were bright and restless. Usually her lids have been drawn down until her eyes were almost closed. Her interest was marked in comparison to the set and stony attitude which she had maintained heretofore."[169]

Prosecutor Weeks called one last witness, Miss Jean Mallock, a 38-year old Mary Poppins type governess who had served Blanca for about six months following the divorce decree. Billy and Maria had hired her through an agency in London and paid for her passage to New York in December 1916. When asked to recall Blanca suffering severe headaches, she did not have a definite answer but bragged of her own home remedy. For all practical purposes, she was a useless witness to either side, but Miss Mallock did provide the best one-liner of the day. She admitted that she had been anxious not to be involved with the case and, until now, had refused to talk to attorneys for the defense.

Miss Mallock announced, in her lilting Scottish accent, "I have a grievance against Mrs. De Saulles and a still larger one against Mr. de Saulles. Does the court wish to know why I'm angry with 'em?"

Spectators bent forward with interest. Reporters poised with their pencils ready to scribble down her next words in shorthand.

Justice Manning looked away and said, "I do not." [170]

The Verdict

In Ancient Greece, the courtesan Phryné was accused of defiling a religious ceremony and was put on trial. If convicted, the punishment would be death. When it seemed the verdict would not be favorable, she stripped off her clothes in court and stood fully nude. The all-male jury gaped in awe of her divine beauty like a marble statue of the goddess Aphrodite brought to life. They forgot the facts of the case and acquitted her of all charges. Two thousand years later, an American court played out virtually the same scene. Blanca de Saulles figuratively stripped herself bare, revealing a tender heart to the jury that won their sympathies and saved her life.

In closing arguments, on a special Saturday session of court, the defense attorney Henry Uterhart emphasized that the only thought on Blanca's mind was taking her son home. He stressed that she could not have premeditated a murder of her ex-husband because she assumed he was not home. Uterhart repeated the testimony of the valet Julius Hadamek who had lied on the telephone to Blanca, saying that John was out. Uterhart argued that by stopping the taxicab a few hundred feet from the house, Blanca did not plan for a quick escape from the scene of a crime but instead had hoped to slip quietly away with her son. Again, he rehashed how miserable she was in her marriage, how lonely she had felt with the inhospitable in-laws in Pennsylvania, and speculated that she transformed herself into a social butterfly to win back her husband's straying affections.

He said, "Is it not perfectly clear that she had found that her real character, simple, sweet, and unspoiled had failed to win the admiration of her husband? She was madly in love with him, she seeks to make herself over into the kind of woman he likes. She has observed that whenever a woman of the Broadway type is present, de Saulles forgets all others and follows her. So she wants to make herself a woman of this kind: the light, vain, frivolous kind that alone attracts men of the stripe of de Saulles." [171]

Uterhart accused John of swindling Blanca out of large sums of money to buy real estate for himself and withhold the profit. He stated that John sold the house on E. 78th Street—supposedly purchased with Blanca's inheritance—and kept all the proceeds for himself. He disputed the child custody schedule and claimed that the boy rightfully belonged with Blanca on the night of August 3rd. He described her mental state as that of a tigress whose little cub had been stolen, saying that her motherhood's basic instinct overpowered the ethics of civilized society. Her ability to act with calm reason was inhibited because of her hypothyroid condition. Supposedly, she fired off her gun without being aware of her actions, in a sort of hormone deficiency intoxication. By the end of this closing argument, every man in the jury had tears in his eyes. The judge adjourned court for fifteen minutes, during which the courtroom observers all sobbed into their handkerchiefs. Even Blanca de Saulles wept publicly for the first time when she stepped out to the corridor for air.

District Attorney Weeks had to follow this melodramatic tsunami with a last-ditch attempt to make it a trial about a person killing someone in cold blood, instead of a trial about John de Saulles's character. His closing argument appealed to common sense, but the people weeping in the courtroom did not hear a word.

"I don't care how bad a man de Saulles was; how he spent his wife's money; I don't care so much how bad his conduct may have been, that does not give the wife the right to shoot him down like a dog." He asked the jury not to be affected by the "sex, beauty, age, position or sympathy of the defendant."

"Has one word of pity or one of regret come from the defendant, or from her witnesses or counsel? Has even decent respect been shown to his relatives? No, it seems that even the family of the dead man cannot be mentioned without a snarl or a hiss, even the aged mother must be referred to discourteously as 'Old Mrs. de Saulles.'"[172]

Judge Manning's instructions to the jury ended with a biblical reference, "Insanity is a defense that requires careful consideration. But if it exists, it has, as I say, gentlemen, the most ancient precept that I can recall, one that we all recall if you will remember the tragedy of Calvary where Christ himself said, 'Father, forgive them, for they know not what they do.' And hence if this woman didn't know what she did you cannot hold her accountable."[173]

Blanca de Saulles's trial laid the groundwork for using medical and scientific expert testimony to defend killers in court. Some of the prosecutor's apparent ineptitude in the de Saulles case can be forgiven; they were forging a path into new territory. Science, forensics, and psychology were just starting to enter the courtroom. The so-called insanity defense was being refined from simple lunacy (upgraded from Satanic possession) to a menu of syndromes tailored by attorneys and expert witnesses to fit the individual defendant and the facts of the case. Charles Weeks had conducted his prosecution as if a Wild West gunfighter stood accused, and he lost to Henry Uterhart's modern legal strategy. As Uterhart wrote later, in *Success in Court*, a collection of essays by nine prominent American trial lawyers, "If I were asked to give 'The Essentials for Success in Court' in a few words, I would answer, 'Complete and Adequate Preparation.' Lawyers win their cases as much in their libraries as in Court..."[174]

The jury deliberated for about three hours, and it only took so long because they had to be meticulous in voting according to the judge's instructions. As they returned to the courtroom, one of them sneaked Blanca a smile and a wink. Everyone saw it. Before the verdict was officially announced, the whole courtroom knew the result. Blanca de Saulles was declared not guilty on December 1, 1917. The clean verdict did not have the rider "by reason of insanity" but completely acquitted her of all blame. She walked out of the courtroom a free woman.

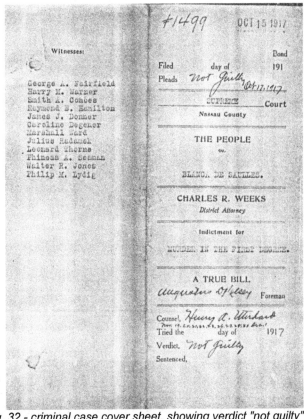

Fig. 32 - criminal case cover sheet, showing verdict "not guilty"

৯৯৩

One by one, the jurors shook her hand and received her smiling thanks. The kindly middle-aged men wished her well and hoped she would get her boy back very soon. Interviewed later, the jurors said that the boy's welfare, and seeing him reunited with his mother, had been their primary motivation.

Charles de Saulles and a few friends left court hastily without speaking to reporters. I can only imagine how crushed they felt—but not entirely surprised—to see Blanca's acquittal being celebrated, to see her smile at the cheering crowds, basking in the applause of feminists. The family would never believe anything else but that it was a cold-blooded premeditated act.

An editorial published in *The Independent* at the time of the de Saulles verdict was titled, "Are Women Above the Law?" and stands out as unique for not glorifying Blanca's maternal instinct as a justification for killing. "...any woman who has a grievance against a man may kill him with impunity.... The trial of a woman for murder or for almost any serious offense in the United States has become a disgraceful farce and a waste of public money. If the American people have no intention of holding a woman accountable before the law, why not say so and be done with it, and amend the statutes accordingly? Let it be understood that the only crime or sin that a woman can commit is to dress unmodishly or unbecomingly, and we shall know what to expect.... It is because The Independent has fearlessly and consistently stood for the rights and opportunities of women, including the right of suffrage, that it feels called upon in the present crisis—for a crisis it is—to use these harsh words. Women must have every educational, industrial and professional opportunity. They must have the right to vote and to hold office. But with these rights they must accept responsibilities and acknowledge the imperative obligation of self-control."[175]

After leaving the courthouse, Blanca drove with her brother and sister to her Long Island home, where she had not been since the night she shot John. Her mother, already told of the verdict by telephone, was resting at "The Crossways" waiting to see her. Blanca's bedroom table was covered with a mountain of messages in all languages sent from the four corners of the earth. The telegraph office in Roslyn, usually quiet and managed by an elderly woman, had been overloaded to the point that the operator asked for help from neighboring towns.

Two days later, the de Saulles family surprised Blanca by delivering little Jack into her arms. Louisa Heckscher, the boy's guardian the last few months, said, "Good-bye, forever" before letting him go. The boy dressed in a sailor's costume still wore the sheriff's badge that had been given to him at the jail. Reporters snapped a few photographs of him sitting on his mother's lap, then he happily went inside the house for a cup of chocolate with his aunt Amalia.

Blanca told reporters gathered on her porch that she intended to stay in the United States and would continue to live at "The Crossways." She praised the courts and said that she had no plans for taking the boy to Chile where he risked losing his citizenship. She insisted that she would bring up her son as an American... a North American like his father. In reality, that promise did not last long.

Aftermath

In folklore, the Woman in White is a sorrowful and sometimes vengeful spirit, the ghost of an innocent woman wronged in life usually by a betrayal of a husband or fiancée. She drifts in lonely places, mourning and weeping into the mist. In Stephen Crane's short story, "The Ghostly Sphinx of Metedeconk" she dooms any man wandering alone, those who are unfortunate enough to encounter her in the fog. In tales from Scotland or France, the White Lady cannot rest in the afterlife, tormented by the sorrows of what has been done to her and what she has done.

❧❧❧

The Family de Saulles

John's father Arthur B. de Saulles died on Christmas Eve, December 24, 1917 a few weeks after Blanca's acquittal. His obituary blamed the stress of witnessing his son's murder and the trial that exonerated Blanca for hastening his end. He was 77 years old.

Little Jack turned five years old the day after his grandfather died, only now he was with Blanca. The aunts and cousins who had cared for the little boy in the last few months were deprived of his cheerful company. They had lost John in an act of senseless violence. Now his cherished son—the only remnant left behind—was taken from them, too. That year was the darkest Christmas season they had ever known.

The family soldiered on with managing their affairs. As the last surviving son, Charles continued his father's business in smelting zinc and also became administrator to his brother's estate. John had started to draw up a will codifying the terms of the divorce and division of property, but he never had the chance to get it signed. After a lengthy probate appraisal process, the debts (including a mortgage and unpaid renovations on "The Box") exceeded the assets by a deficit of more than $23,000[176] and so the widow Blanca and little Jack were left with nothing. The Long Island home, the scene of the tragic shooting, went into foreclosure and sold a year later at auction.[177]

Marshall E. Ward continued his Wall Street wheeling-and-dealing. In the early 1920s, his financial firm of Einstein, Ward & Co. was suspended from the New York Stock Exchange because of unethical practices only a year after being admitted and eventually went bankrupt[178]. He represents the sort of high stakes shenanigans that led up to the stock market crash in 1929 and the Great Depression. He died unmarried and alone, of heart disease, on August 13, 1937 at a hospital in Queens, New York.[179]

Julius Hadamek, the valet, lived a good long life and found true love. He married a dependable Swedish woman, close to his own age, in New York City on August 1, 1919, almost two years to the day after John de Saulles's murder. As of the 1920 federal

250

census, Julius and Olive Hadamek lived at 202 W. 88th Street in Manhattan and he continued to work as a chauffeur. According to his 1922 passport application that is rich with handwritten notes of the immigration officer, Julius was originally a native of Austria born 12 April 1880 the son of Otto Hadamek. He emigrated out of Cherbourg, France in November 1909[180] and settled in New York City. A few years after the de Saulles tragedy, Julius became a naturalized citizen at the court of New York in January 1921. The following year, he and his wife Olive applied for their first U.S. passports in order to travel to Europe to visit relatives in Austria and Sweden. Physically, he was somewhat small, about 5 feet 5 inches, with dark hair and brown eyes. His passport photograph looks stern and sad, although to be fair, no one looks good in such things. Julius and Olive were still together 20 years later when he filled out his compulsory World War II draft registration card in April 1942. As far as I know, Julius was faithful to his master John de Saulles for the rest of his life. He did not attempt to cash in by writing his memoirs or speaking to the newspapers. Except for his testimony in court, he did not talk about any of it. Whatever he knew about Joan Sawyer, Blanca de Saulles, Valentino, or the night John was shot... he took it all to the grave.

Maurice Heckscher and his wife Louisa had cared for little Jack throughout the trial, welcoming the boy into their home along with their four small children: Frances, Nancy, August, and baby

Maurice Jr.[181] Soon after Blanca's acquittal, the real estate company of Heckscher & de Saulles dissolved and its assets were acquired by Cushman & Wakefield, Inc. a newly organized corporation.[182] Maurice continued for several years as a member of the board of directors until the stock market crash of 1929 did them in, too. Maurice maintained his lifestyle in high society, traveling annually to California to participate in polo matches at country clubs.[183] Yet he fell "off the wagon" during the Prohibition era and scandalized the family name in the newspapers by being seen in the company of other women. Louisa divorced him in May 1927 through the Paris court system to avoid New York's restrictive laws. He did not fight for custody of their four children; he simply surrendered. Maurice remarried four months later to a silent film actress Luella Gear, then after a few years divorced her in Reno. He married a third time to Dorothy Bennett[184] and lived into his 80s when he died in June 1967.

The youngest of his sons Maurice Heckscher Jr.—a talented writer and budding newspaperman—died of spinal meningitis in April 1944 while at army training camp. Congenial and well-liked by his peers, "Maury" was the camp's morale officer. Verses of a poem he had written in his school days are quoted in a memorial book archived on the website of St. Paul's School: "Seek not too eagerly to come of age, / Ask not impatiently all things to know, / Lest in your hurrying you lose these years, / And fail to grieve their passing when they go."[185]

Maurice's other son August Heckscher, named for his grandfather, became a successful journalist and newspaper editor, the New York City Parks Commissioner in the 1960s and advisor to President John F. Kennedy. He served at the head of the Woodrow Wilson Foundation that is the main repository of archive materials. Drawing upon years of research and thousands of documents, August Heckscher wrote a biography of Woodrow Wilson in 1991 that is generally cited as the best authority on Wilson's life and presidency. August's book is meticulous and thorough except for one small omission; it does not mention his cousin John de Saulles and gives only a brief passing nod to the academic community's support during the 1912 election.

John's mother Catherine de Saulles died in 1928 at the age of 87 and is buried in historic Green-wood Cemetery in Brooklyn, not far from where her son is interred.[186] John's older sister Georgiana Armide McClintock died in 1933 at age 61, followed by her husband Garrison McClintock in 1939. Rudolph Degener died of a heart attack in 1937 at his coconut plantation near Trinidad in the West Indies, but his wife Caroline—John's younger sister and witness to his shooting—lived until 1964. She was the last of the original siblings.

Charles de Saulles's grief and outrage apparently poisoned an already shaky marriage. He divorced Louise and remarried to a much younger woman. With Anne Barnetz, he had a third son Norman L. de Saulles. As of the 1930 federal census, he lived at 425 East 51st Street in Manhattan, New York and also maintained ownership of "The Box" in honor of his brother's memory.[187] Charles lived until 1962 and passed away in New York at the age of 85. He is buried in Green-wood Cemetery in Brooklyn in the same plot (Lot 9460, Section 45) side by side for all eternity with his brother John.

💥

The Family Errázuriz

In January 1918, Blanca took her son to Honolulu, Hawaii for a vacation while back on the mainland her lawyers worked to settle her affairs. Three months after her acquittal, the court granted her full custody of John de Saulles Jr. She wasted no time continuing westward across the Pacific Ocean and settled in Tokyo, Japan for a while.[188] At the time, Japan was an exotic and glamorous place having opened its gates to the West only fifty years before. The artwork of the samurai days had inspired the French impressionists, and the kimono influenced the silhouette of designer fashions. On a more practical level, Japan was in a boom of expansion—its own Industrial Revolution—quickly

254

transforming its fishing villages into major seaports with the construction of steamships, railroads, telephone and telegraph. In the first world war, Japan was an ally of Britain and played a key role in preventing German advances in the Pacific arena.

World War One ended with the signing of the Armistice in November of 1918, in the midst of a catastrophic global flu pandemic. Blanca and her son Jacky, untouched by the deadly flu, returned home to her family in Chile where she would remain for the rest of her life.

The Chilean poet Manuel Magallanes Moure visited Blanca's widowed mother Doña Blanca in Viña del Mar in February 1918—not long after the verdict—and described the refined and dignified spirit of this old-school aristocrat. The poet spoke of her mood as joyous and serene, full of relief that her daughter had been saved from the gallows. Doña Blanca enjoyed the pleasures of her Venetian style villa, her exotic cloistered garden, the sunshine and the mild sea breezes by the coast, a cultured life of classical music and European style art, and the company of her gentle friends. Over the years, she would be hostess to a number of foreign dignitaries including Ferdinand of Bourbon and Bavaria in 1920, the Prince of Wales (future King Edward VIII) in 1925, and the Hindu guru Krishnamurti who came to share her half-pagan, half-mystical love of beautiful things. Yet in this exquisite paradise, she was a solitary figure—the lone survivor of everyone else in her immediate family.

About five years later, in May 1922, Blanca's brother Guillermo Errázuriz committed suicide. A false story appeared in the newspapers that he killed himself over an infatuation with Peggy Joyce, the actress who ironically played the Joan Sawyer role in a silent film loosely based on the de Saulles murder trial. Miss Joyce gave interviews sobbing in her satin negligee and detailed the whole sordid tale of what happened with "poor Billy," that while partying all night in Paris cabarets with her, he drunkenly declared his undying love. She claims she turned him down flat, saying they were just friends, humiliating him in front of everybody. The only true part of her story comes at the end: he walked into his adjoining hotel room and shot himself.[189] He left behind his wife Maria Edwards and his four-year old daughter.

The Errázuriz family denied the actress's story immediately and denounced Peggy Joyce for seeking publicity to promote her career in motion pictures.[190] Billy's brother-in-law Agustin Edwards (author, newspaperman, and President of the General Assembly of the League of Nations) spoke on behalf of the family. He explained that a suicide note from Billy clearly stated that money troubles—not an obsession with the actress—had compelled him to take his own life. Billy's friend Henri Letellier also denied Peggy Joyce's story that they had quarreled over her in a love triangle, calling her version of events "utterly fantastic," and insisted that he and Billy were friends on the best of terms. Agustin Edwards asked the reporters to respect the family in their time of grief, which of course did not happen.

After Billy's suicide, his wife Maria remained in Paris as a widow. Years later, during the Nazi occupation, she joined the French Resistance and helped to rescue Jewish children separated from their parents and on their way to concentration camps. She was arrested, interrogated and tortured by the Gestapo several times, but her diplomatic relations engineered her escape. In September 1953 she received the Legion of Honor award in France. For her courage and sacrifice, Maria Errázuriz was posthumously honored in November 2005 by Israel's Yad Vashem memorial as #10698, one of the Righteous Among the Nations.

⊱⊰

Blanca married for the second time on December 22, 1921 to a wealthy Chilean man named Fernando Santa Cruz Wilson[191]. The wedding took place a few days before her son little Jack's ninth birthday. By marrying again, she officially lost her U.S. citizenship and became a Chilean national once more. Her second husband, a senator in Chile's parliament, was also from an illustrious family of politicians. Fernando, two months younger than Blanca, was a civil engineer and a former *alcade* (mayor) of

San Rafael de Pocochay in the region of La Cruz. This is the sort of fellow she would have married if John de Saulles had not come along.

Blanca made two more visits to New York, now as Mrs. Blanca de Santa Cruz the wife of a diplomat. Once in December 1936 she was accompanied by Agustin Edwards or perhaps she was his guest. For the last time in November 1937, she sailed alone out of Cherbourg, France on a diplomatic visa. On that final arrival at Ellis Island, she listed her old friend D. Stewart Iglehart as her destination contact person. Stewart's wife Aida, a childhood friend of Blanca's, had passed away in 1933 but apparently Blanca stayed in touch. His son Stewart Iglehart Jr.—about the same age as little Jackie—was a champion international polo player with a home base at the Meadow Brook club. Her visit in the U.S. only lasted for two weeks and she sailed for home aboard the steamship *Santa Clara*.[192]

A rare photograph taken of Blanca in the mid-1930s shows her dressed in chic style *à la* Greta Garbo and smiling from a banquet table at a black-tie social event. Sitting next to his mother is an adult John de Saulles Jr. with a moustache, as a slender debonair fellow in a tuxedo. Blanca is thrilled to have her picture taken; Jackie appears bored or impatient for the photographer to finish his business and move along.

Fig. 33 - Blanca Errázuriz and her son John L. de Saulles, Jr. (circa 1932-1935)

Blanca would not live to see the United States enter into the Second World War. On March 20, 1940, Blanca died at her home in Viña del Mar after what the *New York Times* called a long illness[193], or what *Newsweek* called heart disease,[194] but the actual cause of death is said to be a barbiturate overdose.[195] Whether it was accidental or suicide is anyone's guess, as only Blanca herself knew what ghosts haunted her mind in those final hours. "¿Eres tu, Jack...?" Blanca was only 46 years old when she died, a few weeks short of her next birthday. In three brief paragraphs, the *Times* obituary summarized the romance that ended later in a divorce, a shooting, a sensational trial, and pondered if her killing of John de Saulles was premeditated murder.

John de Saulles Jr. (a.k.a. Jaime Errázuriz) never married or had children. At age fifty-something, he collapsed and died of a heart attack while playing golf.

෧෪

The Woman and The Law (1918)

Hollywood rushed to produce a silent film in 1918, *The Woman and The Law* starring Jack Connors, Miriam Cooper, and Peggy Joyce. The movie made a weak attempt to pass itself off as fiction, renaming the main characters as Mr. and Mrs. Jack La Salle, but the film's promotional ads and reviews clearly make the connection. "The struggle of a woman for her child and the lengths to which she will go for its protection are picturized [sic] with tremendous dramatic intensity... Based on the internationally sensational de Saulles case, which so shocked the United States and South America and which was discussed in every home in the country, it is said, the thrilling moment when the woman who has slain for the sake of her child faces the jury which is to decide her fate, depicts a situation to hold the most hardened play-goer spellbound."[196]

*Fig. 34 - A promotional still photograph of actress Miriam Cooper
from the film The Woman and the Law (1918)*

The actress Miriam Cooper had such an uncanny resemblance to the real Blanca de Saulles that people often stopped her on the street. The film is pure exploitation that paints Blanca's character as a heroine who loved her child above all things and would do anything to protect him. Apparently, the early scenes in the film depict her playing tenderly with dolls to foreshadow her intense maternal instincts. Her cheating husband engaged in mediocre tango dancing as a promiscuous scoundrel who deserved what he got.

The film had international distribution and played as *La Mujer y La Ley* at the Olympic Theatre in Blanca's home town of Viña del Mar. Theater-goers in Chile expected a film to reveal details from the North American perspective that had not appeared in the censored local press, but they came away disappointed and highly offended. Many of them personally knew Blanca de Saulles and the Errázuriz family who lived in the mansion on the other side of town. Their magnificent country was represented as a primitive wilderness of Florida palm trees and beaches. The stately matriarch Doña Blanca was inaccurately was portrayed as a Spanish señora with a ridiculous *mantilla* comb in her hair. Ticket sales lagged and the film inevitably was packed away in its aluminum cans. Like so many silent movies, the fragile nitrate reels crumbled to dust within a couple of years and no copies are known to exist. All that remains are newspaper reviews and a few publicity photographs.

Rudolph Nureyev as Valentino (1977)

The characters of John and Blanca de Saulles were portrayed on film once again in 1977, in a few brief scenes in Ken Russell's wildly exaggerated bio-drama *Valentino* starring ballet dancer Rudolph Nureyev in the title role. Blanca first appears dipping the tango in a supper club with "Rudy" and her very blonde, jealous husband breaks them up. John de Saulles insults the gigolo by stuffing dollar bills into the handkerchief pocket of his tuxedo as if it's a stripper's G-string. In the next scene, Blanca visits Rudy's apartment where he is boiling spaghetti. She brings along her toddler son, dressed in a sailor's suit; I guess the nanny was busy that day. Just as she and Rudy are about to kiss, her abusive husband barges into the room. There is much screaming and hugging of the baby as Rudy gets punched with brass knuckles, followed by a quick scene of John de Saulles enjoying a fit of cruel laughter until Blanca pulls a pistol from her white fur muff and shoots him in the face. There is nothing of the divorce or the murder trial; the whole episode is over-simplified and condensed. Blanca makes her exit weeping hysterically on the run from a mob of paparazzi.

❧

Legacy of the Woman in White

Seven years after the killing of John de Saulles, the 1924 trial of murder partners Nathan Leopold and Richard Loeb is generally recognized as setting the precedent for claiming an abusive childhood as an excuse for a violent crime. In other words, it wasn't their fault for being psychopathic murderers because they were messed up as children. Their mental and moral damage made them social cripples unable to distinguish between right and wrong. Surely the famous defense attorney Clarence Darrow had followed the de Saulles trial and learned from Mr. Uterhart's strategy of dramatizing a defendant's past history of abuse (real or exaggerated) to evade responsibility for a violent act.

An editorial published in *The Independent* at the time of the de Saulles verdict was titled, "Are Women Above the Law?" and stands out as unique for not glorifying Blanca's maternal instinct as a justification for killing. "...any woman who has a grievance against a man may kill him with impunity.... The trial of a woman for murder or for almost any serious offense in the United States has become a disgraceful farce and a waste of public money. If the American people have no intention of holding a woman accountable before the law, why not say so and be done with it, and amend the statutes accordingly? Let it be understood that the only crime or sin that a woman can commit is to dress unmodishly or unbecomingly, and we shall know what to expect.... It is because The Independent has fearlessly and consistently stood for the rights and opportunities of women, including the right of suffrage, that it feels called upon in the present crisis—for a crisis it is—to use these harsh words. Women must have every educational, industrial and professional opportunity. They must have the right to vote and to hold office. But with these rights they must accept responsibilities and acknowledge the imperative obligation of self-control."[197]

After her daughter's death in 1940, the elderly Doña Blanca sold the family estate to the municipality of Viña del Mar and donated numerous oil paintings and garden sculptures to what is today Quinta Vergara Park. For many years, the aging widow had been a patron of artists, so it seemed a natural progression that she would convert her palatial mansion into a museum and a school of fine arts.

Today, the gardens are maintained long after Doña Blanca has ceased to stroll the floral paths. An impressive outdoor amphitheater was built in the 1960s, and renovated in 2002, that is the site of an annual music festival (*Festival Internacional de la Canción de Viña del Mar*) where international headliners such as Julio Iglesias, Sting, and Olivia Newton-John have performed. It is considered one of the premier concert venues in the world. Ultimately, this is the legacy of the Woman in White: that gentleness, beauty, and a joy of living can emerge from tragedy, violence, and pain.

About the Author

Denise B. Tanaka works as a paralegal in the challenging field of U.S. immigration law. She has a passion for historical research and a decades-long genealogy habit. A resident of the western United States, she shares her life with a husband from Japan and two daughters who are her inspiration.

Twitter: @DeniseBTanaka

BIBLIOGRAPHY

Original Rare and Archived Documents

People of the State of New York v. Blanca de Saulles. Supreme Court Nassau County, Mineola, New York. Criminal indictment. October 15, 1917

Archibald Johnston Letterbook 1912, University Library SC MS 0137, Special Collections, Linderman Library, Lehigh University, Bethlehem, PA.

Baptismal Certificate, John Longer de Saulles Jr., baptized January 6, 1913. Original certificate issued by Holy Infancy Church, Bethlehem, PA. June 22, 2011.

de Saulles, John L., Treasurer. "Request for Contributions," Woodrow Wilson College Men's League, 7th in Volume. 1912. Special Collections SAL3, Cecil H. Green Library, Stanford University, Palo Alto, CA.

de Saulles, John Longer – Former Yale Quarterback. "How to Play Quarterback," in Spalding's How to Play Football - A Primer on the Modern College Game with Tactics Brought Down to Date. Spalding's Athletic Library No. 210, edited by Walter Camp, new edition revised for 1904. Courtesy of Abraham Lincoln Presidential Library, Springfield, IL.

Death Certificate, Arthur Percy de Saulles, April 3, 1896. Original certificate issued by New Jersey State Archives, Trenton, NJ. June 8, 2011.

John L. de Saulles letters to and from Colonel Edward Mandell House, Edward Mandell House Papers 1913 - 1914, MS 466, Box 37, Folder 1173. Manuscripts and Archives, Sterling Memorial Library, Yale University, New Haven, CT.

Books

"Biography of Major Arthur B. DeSaulles," in Biographical and Portrait Cyclopedia of Fayette County, Pennsylvania, Chicago, IL: John M. Gresham & Co. 1889.

"Biography of Major Arthur B. DeSaulles," in Biographical and Portrait Cyclopedia of Fayette County, Pennsylvania. Philadelphia, PA: L.H. Everts & Co. 1882.

Bailey, Lee with Ella Brennan, Lee Bailey's New Orleans, Good Food and Glorious Houses. New York: Clarkson Potter/Publishers. 1993.

Brainard, W.F. Who's Who in New York City and State, A Biographical Dictionary of Contemporaries. Fifth Biennial Edition. Press of Wm. G. Hewitt, Brooklyn, NY. 1911

Caistor, Nick. In Focus—Chile, A Guide to the People, Politics and Culture. New York: Interlink Books. 1998.

Carson, Woodward Christian. South Bethlehem, Pennsylvania, 1880 - 1920, Industrialization, Immigration and the Development of a Religious Landscape. Master of Science thesis, University of Pennsylvania. 2000.

Castagneto, Piero. Una Historia de Viña del Mar. Santiago, Chile: RIL Editores. 2010.

Castagneto, Piero. Viña del Mar: Una Mirada Historica, Turistica y Patrimonial. A Historical, Touristic, and Cultural View. Viña del Mar, Chile: Unidad de Patrimonio. 2008

Chace, James. 1912: Wilson, Roosevelt, Taft & Debs—the Election that Changed the Country. New York: Simon & Schuster. 2004.

Collier, Simon and William F. Sater. A History of Chile, 1808-1994. Cambridge, MA: Cambridge University Press. 1996.

Corks and Curls, University of Virginia Yearbook. Albert & Shirley Small Special Collections Library, University of Virginia, Charlottesville, VA. 1903.

Council of the Chi Phi Fraternity. The Chi Phi Register, ed. by Arthur G. Thompson, Grand Alpha. New York, 1908.

Edwards, Agustin. My Native Land: Panorama, Reminiscences, Writers and Folklore, London: Ernest Benn Ltd. 1928.

Floyd, Nancy. She's Got a Gun. Philadelphia: Temple University Press. 2008.

Foot Ball Rules: As Recommended by the Rules Committee. ed. by Walter Camp. Spalding Co. 1902.

Forbes, Bertie Charles – Editor of Forbes Magazine. Men Who are Making America. B.C. Forbes Publishing Co. 1st ed. Dec. 1917, 2nd ed. Mar. 1918.

Friedman, Lawrence. A History of American Law, 3rd ed. New York: A Touchstone Book, Simon & Schuster. 2005.

Genealogical and Family History of Southern New York and The Hudson River Valley. Vol. I, New York Lewis Historical Publishing Co. 1913. Transcribed manually by Holice B. Young, for the Mardos Memorial On-Line Library of Historical Publications, D. J. Coover, Webmaster. *www.ustphistor@usgennet.org*

Giblin, Harold. "Early Aviators, Biographical Notes - Harold S. Fowler." Unfinished book manuscript, uploaded to website of The Early Birds of

Aviation, Inc. maintained by Ralph Cooper.
http://earlyaviators.com/efowharo.htm

Halsey, Frederic M. (Frederic Magie). Railway expansion in Latin America; descriptive and narrative history of the railroad systems of Argentina, Peru, Venezuela, Brazil, Chile, Bolivia and all other countries of South and Central America. New York, NY: The Moody Magazine and Book Company. 1916.

Heckscher, August. Woodrow Wilson: A Biography, New York, NY: Charles Scribner's Sons. 1991.

In the Service: Workers on the Grand Estates of Long Island 1890s – 1940s. ed. by Elly Shodell. New York, NY: Port Washington Public Library. 1991.

Janis, Elsie. So Far, So Good!: An Autobiography. New York: E.P. Dutton & Co., Inc. 1932.

Kirwin, Barbara R., Ph.D. The Mad, the Bad, and the Innocent: The Criminal Mind on Trial—Tales of a Forensic Psychologist. Little, Brown & Co. 1997.

La Cuidad, Un Espacio Educativo, Guia Metodologica. Viña del Mar, Chile: Unidad de Patrimonio. 2007.

Larrain, Luz. Blanca Elena: Memoria Indiscreta de la Quinta Vergara. Santiago, Chile: Editorial Sudamericana. 1994.

Leider, Emily W. Dark Lover: the Life and Death of Rudolph Valentino, New York, NY: Farrar, Straus and Giroux. 2003.

Markham, George. Guns of the Wild West. Firearms of the American Frontier 1849 - 1917. London: Arms & Armour Press. 1991.

Massey, Lea, and Heckscher Families, ed. by Alexander duBin. Philadelphia, PA: Historical Publication Society. 1948.

Medina, Jose Toribio. Los Errázuriz: notas biograficas y documentos para la historia de esta familia en Chile. Adiciones y ampliaciones por Carlos J. Larrain. Santiago, Chile: Editorial Universitaria. 1964.

Montgomery Ward & Co. Catalogue and Buyers Guide, No. 57 Spring and Summer, 1895. An unabridged reprint of the original edition with a new introduction by Boris Emmet. New York, NY: Dover Publications, Inc. 1969.

New York Social Blue Book – 1930. Transcribed to Brooklyn Genealogy, www.bklyn-genealogy-info.com

Plath, Oreste. El Santiago Que Se Fue. Santiago, Chile: Editorial Grijalbo S.A. 1997

Randall, Monica. The Mansions of Long Island's Gold Coast. New York: Hasting House Publishers. 1979.

Ried, Alberto. El Mar Trajo Mi Sangre. Santiago, Chile: Editorial del Pacifico S.A. 1956.

Shankweiler, Fred L. with Frank T. Boyle. Men of Bethlehem. Bethlehem, PA. 1918

Standard Corporation Service, Daily Revised, Standard Statistics Company, Inc. 1915.

Trimpi, Helen P. Crimson Confederates, Harvard Men Who Fought for the South. Knoxville, TN: University of Tennessee Press. 2010.

University of Virginia: Its History, Influence, Equipment and Characteristics. Biographical Sketches and Portraits of Founders, Benefactors, Officers and Alumni. New York, NY. Vol. II, 1904.

Uterhart, Henry. Essay titled, "Henry A. Uterhart," in Success in Court, ed. by Francis L. Wellman. New York, NY: The MacMillan Co. 1941.

Waugh, Daisy. Last Dance with Valentino, New York and U.K.: Harper-Collins. 2011.

Weidman, Bette S., and Linda B. Martin. Nassau County Long Island In Early Photographs, 1869 – 1940. New York, NY: Courier Dover Publications. 1981.

Werner, Joseph H. Inhabitants of Northampton County as furnished by the Census Bureau at Washington, D.C. in the Eleventh U. S. Census, 1890. Transcribed to Bethlehem PA Online. www.bethlehempaonline.com

Wharton, Edith. The Age of Innocence, Collier Books, 1993. Originally published in 1920 by D. Appleton & Company.

Wilson, J. and Son. Report of the Class of 1857 in Harvard College, Prepared for the Twenty-Fifth Anniversary of Its Graduation. 1882.

Periodicals

"Are Women Above the Law?" in *The Independent.* Independent Publications, Inc. Editors: Leonard Bacon, Joseph Parrish Thompson, Richard Salter Storrs, Henry Ward Beecher, Joshua Leavitt, Henry Chandler Bowen, Theodore Tilton, William Hays Ward, Hamilton Holt, Harold de Wolf Fuller, Fabian Franklin, Christian Archibald Herter. Volume 92, p. 499, 1917.

"Biographical Notes," obituary of Arthur B. de Saulles, in *AIME Transactions.* Vol. 61, January 1, 1920.

"Charles Augustus Heckscher de Saulles," in *Decennial Record, Yale University Sheffield Scientific School, Class of 1899.* p. 76. The Tuttle, Morehouse & Taylor Co., 1910.

"Died: Blanca Errázuriz de Santa Cruz." *Newsweek.* April 1, 1940

"Entregaran Condecoracion a Chilena que Salvo a Niños Judios en Paris," *La Palabra Israelita.* Nov. 3, 2006.

"La Tragedia de Mineola." *El Grafico*, vol. II, No. 3, page 444. New York, NY. January 1918.

"Obituary: Louis de Saulles Jr." *Coal Age*, Vol. 8, MacLean Hunter Publishing Co. 1915, page 481

"Paterson Signs No-Fault Divorce Bill," *New York Times.* New York, NY. August 15, 2010

"The Skyscraper Times, vol. 4, No. 5," December 1917. Reproduced in *Buildings* Volume 17, National Convention of Building Managers, Stamats Pub. Co., 1917.

"Valentino's Lost Tango," anonymous interview with author Daisy Waugh, *London Sunday Times*, London (UK) magazine insert, Jan. 16, 2011.

Dershowitz, Alan M. "Wives Also Kill Husbands—Quite Often." Excerpt from *The Abuse Excuse: And Other Cop-Outs, Sob Stories and Evasions of Responsibility.* Boston: Little Brown. 1994.

Gibbs, Nancy. "Sex, Lies, Arrogance: What Makes Powerful Men Behave So Badly?" *TIME* magazine. May 19, 2011.

Maino, Valeria P. and Mireya Redondo M. "Los X en la Quinta Vergara." *Archivum*, The Journal of the Historical Heritage Archive of Viña del Mar. Year V, No. 6. Unidad de Patrimonio, Viña del Mar, Chile. 2004.

New York Society for the Prevention of Cruelty to Children, 125th Anniversary 1875-2000. Commemorative anniversary pamphlet, NYSPCC. New York: NY. 2000.

Sacks, Benjamin, Ph. D. "The Duchess of Windsor and The Coronado Legend, Part II," by *The Journal of San Diego History, San Diego Historical Society Quarterly*, Winter 1988, Vol. 34, No. 1. Thomas L. Scharf, Editor.

Shields, Jody. "The Queen Of Clean," *New York Times*, Home Design Magazine. October 11, 1992.

Vergara, Blanca K. "Salvador Vergara: Remembranzas de su Nieta." *Archivum*, The Journal of the Historical Heritage Archive of Viña del Mar. Year V, No. 6. Unidad de Patrimonio, Viña del Mar, Chile. 2004.

Legal Reference Sources

in re. de Saulles. New York State Reporter, NY Supp., vol. 167 p. 445. West Publishing. 1918.

People v. Alfred Daly, Trial #2145, New York Court of General Sessions, charged with "keeping a disorderly house." Judge Otto Rosalsky. Jan. 12, 1916. Trial Transcripts, Court of General Sessions 1883 - 1927, archived at Lloyd Sealy Library, John Jay College of Criminal Justice, New York, NY.

Saulles v. Percy Mining Co. Court of Common Pleas, Fayette County, Pennsylvania. Pittsburgh Legal Journal. July 26, 1906

Ward v. Paul J. Rainey Pier Co. New York State Reporter, NY Supp., 134 N.Y. S. 245, 149 App. Div. 707. West Publishing. 1912.

Websites

Errázuriz Winery, Chile. http://www.errazuriz.cl/errazuriz/english/vina.html

Genealogia de Chile, family trees and articles about prominent families of Chile, compiled and maintained by Mauricio Pelleux Cepeda (in Spanish) www.genealog.cl

Green-wood Cemetery, Brooklyn, New York. www.green-wood.com

Heckscher Museum of Art, Huntington, NY www.heckscher.org

Historic Long Island, New York. www.historiclongisland.com

La Red Maestros de Maestros, a schoolteachers' networking site sponsored by Chile's Ministry of Education. Escuela Hugo Errázuriz No. 24, Viña del Mar. www.rmm.cl

Larchmont Historical Society, Larchmont, NY www.larchmonthistory.org

Long Beach Island Landmarks Association, New York www.lbila.homestead.com

Meadowbrook Polo Club History, Long Island, NY. www.meadowbrookpolo.com

Museum of the City of New York, NY. http://www.mcny.org/

Port of New York Ellis Island, online database of passenger arrival lists and ship manifests. The Statue of Liberty-Ellis Island Foundation, Inc. www.ellisisland.org

South Bethlehem Historical Society, Pennsylvania www.southbethhistsoc.org

U.S. Citizenship & Immigration Services. www.uscis.gov

U.S. Department of State. www.state.gov

U.S. Geological Survey, database of historical earthquakes worldwide www.usgs.gov

U.S. Patent & Trademarks Office, www.uspto.gov

Unidad de Patrimonio, Chile. The municipality of Viña del Mar. www.patrimoniovina.cl

Walter Camp Football Foundation, www.waltercamp.org

Yad Vashem, Holocaust Martyrs and Heroes Remembrance Authority www.yadvashem.org

Historical Archived Newspapers

Cass City Chronicle – Cass City, MI
Day Book – Chicago, IL
El Paso Herald – El Paso, TX
Evening Public Ledger – Philadelphia, PA
Evening World – New York, NY
Medford Mail Tribune – Medford, OR
New Orleans Daily Picayune – New Orleans, LA
New York Times – New York, NY
New York Tribune – New York, NY
Ogden Standard – Ogden, UT
San Francisco Call – San Francisco, CA
San Francisco Chronicle – San Francisco, CA
San Jose Mercury News – San Jose, CA
Tacoma Times – Tacoma, WA
The Sun – New York, NY
Times Dispatch – Richmond, VA
Washington Times – Washington D.C.

List of Figures

Fig.	Source
15	Edward Mandell House Papers. Manuscripts and Archives, Yale University Library
16	Edward Mandell House Papers. Manuscripts and Archives, Yale University Library
17	Bain News Service, LOC, LC-B2- 3527-3 [P&P]
18	Bain News Service, LOC, LCB2 274014 [P&P]
19	Library of Congress, Lot 3788 - Box 4 [item] [P&P]
20	Wikimedia Commons, original held at Dixon Gallery and Gardens, Memphis, Tennessee
21	New York World-Telegram & Sun collection, LOC, Reference Section, Prints and Photographs Division
22	Advertisement for O'Sullivan's Heels with endorsement by Joan Sawyer. Source: April 1915 issue of *The Theatre* magazine. Author's personal collection.
23	Bain News Service, LOC, LC-B2- 6477-3 [P&P]
24	New York World-Telegram & Sun collection, LOC, Reference Section, Prints and Photographs Division
25	New York World-Telegram & Sun collection, LOC, Reference Section, Prints and Photographs Division
26	copy of original document, courtesy of the county court of Nassau County, Mineola, New York
27	Bain News Service, LOC, LC-B2- 4055-17 [P&P]
28	Bain News Service, LOC, LC-B2-4055-16 [P&P]
29	Bain News Service, LOC, LC-B2- 3269-7 [P&P]
30	Bain News Service, LOC, LC-B2- 4055-12 [P&P]
31	New York World-Telegram & Sun collection, LOC, Reference Section, Prints and Photographs Division
32	copy of original document, courtesy of the county court of Nassau County, Mineola, New York

Fig.   **Source**

33   courtesy of the private collection of author Daisy Waugh,
        reprinted from "Valentino's Lost Tango," *London Sunday
        Times*, London (UK) magazine insert, Jan. 16, 2011.

34   Wikimedia Commons, original source unknown

NOTES

[1] *Football Days*, 1916, p. 348

[2] *Spalding's Rules of Football*, 1902 ed., page 59

[3] This date 1902 is an error because he had graduated Yale before the fall of that year.

[4] *Washington Times*, Yale Crushed by Harvard, Nov. 24, 1901

[5] *New York Times*, Yale Quarterback Recovered, Nov. 25, 1901

[6] *San Francisco Call*, "Coley" Carnegie Will Become Laird of Skibo, June 30, 1906

[7] *The Times-Dispatch*, Virginia, A Loving Cup for Coach de Saulles, March 15, 1903

[8] Corks and Curls, University of Virginia yearbook, 1903, p. 134 – 137

[9] *The Times*, Virginia, Excellent Prospects: Coach de Saulles Thinks the N.C. Game will help Va. Next Year, Dec. 30, 1902

[10] Spalding's 1904, page 89

[11] Spalding's 1904, page 93 - 95

[12] Spalding's 1904, page 89 - 90

[13] Spalding's 1904, page 91

[14] Walter Camp Football Foundation website

[15] Spalding's 1904, page 95

[16] Paris death notices

[17] *New York Times*, De Saulles Boy Given to Mother, Dec. 3, 1917

[18] Desc_Libro_Vina 2008, <u>Viña del Mar: Una Mirada Historica, Turistica y Patrimonial. A Historical, Touristic, and Cultural View.</u> 2008. page 42 (photograph)

[19] *New York Times*, Holds De Saulles Drove Wife Mad, Nov. 24, 1917

[20] *The Sun*, New York, Aug. 20, 1905

[21] *New York Times*, Long Beach Hotel Burns at Dawn, July 30, 1907

[22] *New York Times*, Heavy Bookings at All Resorts, June 20, 1909

[23] *New York Times*, Ready to Build New Long Beach Pier, Jan. 12, 1910

[24] 1905 New York State census

[25] *Ward v. Paul J. Rainey Pier Co.*, NY Supp.

[26] Elsie Janis. <u>So Far, So Good!: An Autobiography.</u> New York: E.P. Dutton & Co., Inc. 1932. p. 50 - 51

[27] So Far, So Good! p. 68

[28] So Far, So Good! p. 67

[29] So Far, So Good! p. 69

[30] So Far, So Good! p. 96

[31] *The Evening World*, New York, Moore - de Saulles Troth A Joke, Jan. 18, 1907

[32] *The Sun*, New York, J.L. de Saulles Ire Aroused, Feb. 17, 1910

[33] *New York Times*, De Saulles is Sued by His Chilean Wife, July 28, 1916

[34] Halsey, Frederic M. (Frederic Magie). <u>Railway expansion in Latin America; descriptive and narrative history of the railroad systems of Argentina, Peru, Venezuela, Brazil, Chile, Bolivia and all other countries of South and Central America.</u> New York, NY: The Moody Magazine and Book Company. 1916.

[35] *New York Times*, Oct. 20, 1909

[36] U.S. Passport applications

[37] *New York Tribune*, De Saulles is Sued by His Chilean Wife, July 28, 1916

[38] *New York Times*, Mrs. de Saulles Tells Her Story of the Tragedy, Aug. 6, 1917

[39] *El Paso Herald*, Powerful Influences Seek to Avenge Slaying of de Saulles, Sep. 12, 1917

[40] *New York Times*, John G. de Saulles to Wed in Paris, Dec. 14, 1911

[41] *New York Times*, John G. de Saulles Weds, Dec. 15, 1911

[42] *El Paso Herald*, Powerful Influences Seek to Avenge Slaying of de Saulles, Sept. 12, 1917

[43] *New York Daily Tribune*, Heavy Sales at Show: Auto Manufacturers Report a Flourishing Business, Jan. 12, 1912

[44] *Cass City Chronicle*, July 5, 1912.

[45] *New York Tribune*, Democrats Book Gives T.R.'s Steel Record, Aug. 31, 1912

[46] Fayette County, Pennsylvania Vital Records, 1750-1890
[47] Massey, Lea, and Heckscher Families, ed. by Alexander duBin. Philadelphia, PA: Historical Publication Society. 1948. pp. 12 - 15
[48] 1870 federal census, Pennsylvania "Arthur deSauls"
[49] "Biography of Major Arthur B. DeSaulles," in Biographical and Portrait Cyclopedia of Fayette County, Pennsylvania. Philadelphia, PA: L.H. Everts & Co. 1882. p. 544
[50] "Biography of Major Arthur B. DeSaulles," in Biographical and Portrait Cyclopedia of Fayette County, Pennsylvania, Chicago, IL: John M. Gresham & Co. 1889. p. 598
[51] U.S. Patent & Trademark Office, no. 694,137 (Feb. 25, 1902) and no. 695,376 (March 11, 1902)
[52] "Biographical Notes," in AIME Transactions. Volume 61, January 1, 1920. p. 720
[53] Woodrow Wilson College Men's League, fund-raising pamphlet, page 3
[54] August Heckscher. Woodrow Wilson: A Biography, New York, NY: Charles Scribner's Sons. 1991. page 253
[55] Woodrow Wilson College Men's League pamphlet, page 3
[56] Woodrow Wilson College Men's League pamphlet, page 31
[57] New York Times, Big Wilson Parade for Times Square, Nov. 3, 1912
[58] James Chace. 1912: Wilson, Roosevelt, Taft & Debs—the Election that Changed the Country. New York: Simon & Schuster. 2004. p. 239
[59] original baptismal certificate, Holy Infancy Church, Bethlehem, PA
[60] New York Times, Mrs. de Saulles Tells Story of Husband's Neglect, Nov. 27, 1917
[61] New York Times, Holds De Saulles Drove Wife Mad, Nov. 24, 1917
[62] So Far, So Good! p. 111
[63] New York Times, Mrs. de Saulles Tells Story of Husband's Neglect, Nov. 27, 1917
[64] Washington Times, De Saulles Widow is Unshaken in Story, Nov. 27, 1917
[65] New York Times, Mrs. de Saulles Tells Story of Husband's Neglect, Nov. 27, 1917
[66] New York Times, Mrs. de Saulles Tells Story of Husband's Neglect, Nov. 27, 1917
[67] New York Times, Malone Sworn In; Will Fight Bosses, Nov. 25, 1913
[68] New York Times, Mrs. de Saulles Tells Story of Husband's Neglect, Nov. 27, 1917
[69] New York Times, Mrs. de Saulles Tells Story of Husband's Neglect, Nov. 27, 1917
[70] New York Times, Mrs. de Saulles Tells Her Story of the Tragedy, Aug. 6, 1917
[71] New York Times, Crack Athletes in Indoor Baseball, Feb. 1, 1914
[72] New York Times, University Club Wins, May 8, 1914
[73] New York Tribune, Mi-Careme Activities, March 15, 1914
[74] New York Times, Easter Fete at Waldorf, 14 April 1914
[75] USGenNet.org, cite to page 267, Vol. I, GENEALOGICAL AND FAMILY HISTORY OF SOUTHERN NEW YORK AND THE HUDSON RIVER VALLEY. NEW YORK LEWIS HISTORICAL PUBLISHING CO. 1913. transcribed by Holice B. Young, for the Mardos Memorial On-Line Library of Historical Publications, uploaded to http://www.usgennet.org/usa/topic/historical/southernnewyork/s_ny_title.htm Copyright © 2000 - 2002 D. J. Coover All Rights Reserved Webmaster: D. J. Coover - ustphistor@usgennet.org
[76] New York Times, De Saulles for Uruguay: President's Own Selection of New York Lawyer as Minister, Mar. 11, 1914
[77] Edward Mandell House papers
[78] New York Times, Mrs. de Saulles Tells Story of Husband's Neglect, Nov. 27, 1917
[79] New York Times, Plan Closer Bonds with Latin America, March 22, 1914
[80] New York Times, Holds De Saulles Drove Wife Mad, Nov. 24, 1917
[81] New York Tribune, De Saulles Refuses Diplomatic Post, June 2, 1914
[82] U.S. Dept. of State, Office of the Historian
[83] Edward Mandell House papers, June 3, 1914
[84] Men Who are Making America, 1917, page 191
[85] New York Tribune, De Saulles Buys House: Gets Dwelling in 78th Street, July 19, 1914
[86] "The Queen Of Clean," Jody Shields, New York Times Magazine, Home Design Magazine, 10/11/1992, p6, 0p.

[87] *New York Times*, I Danced, But Not In My Heart, Says Mrs. de Saulles, Nov. 28, 1917

[88] *Washington Times*, De Saulles Widow is Unshaken in Story, Nov. 27, 1917

[89] *New York Times*, Holds De Saulles Drove Wife Mad, Nov. 24, 1917

[90] *New York Times*, Aug. 7, 1914

[91] *New York Times*, Aug. 13, 1914

[92] *New York Times*, Oct. 2, 1914

[93] *New York Times*, Holds De Saulles Drove Wife Mad, Nov. 24, 1917

[94] *Washington Times*, De Saulles Widow is Unshaken in Story, Nov. 27, 1917

[95] Early Aviators, Biographical Notes - Harold S. Fowler, from unfinished book by Harold Giblin, page maintained by Ralph Cooper. http://earlyaviators.com/efowharo.htm

[96] *New York Times*, I Danced, But Not In My Heart, Says Mrs. de Saulles Nov. 28, 1917

[97] *New York Times*, I Danced, But Not In My Heart, Says Mrs. de Saulles Nov. 28, 1917 (Ibid.)

[98] *Washington Times*, De Saulles Widow is Unshaken in Story, Nov. 27, 1917

[99] *New York Times*, I Danced, But Not In My Heart, Says Mrs. de Saulles Nov. 28, 1917

[100] *New York Times*, Insanity Defense Planned to Save Mrs. de Saulles, Aug. 5, 1917

[101] *Standard Corporation Service, Daily Revised*, 1915. page 1192

[102] *New York Times*, Frozen Grounds Delight Players Jan. 9, 1916

[103] *New York Times*, Holds De Saulles Drove Wife Mad, Nov. 24, 1917

[104] *New York Times*, Holds De Saulles Drove Wife Mad, Nov. 24, 1917 (Ibid.)

[105] *New York Times*, I Danced, But Not In My Heart, Says Mrs. de Saulles Nov. 28, 1917

[106] *Dark Lover*, p. 68, quoting a reference to "Valentino: The Life Story of the Sheik," part 2, *Liberty*, September 18, 1929 by Adela Rogers St. Johns.

[107] *New York Times*, I Danced, But Not In My Heart, Says Mrs. de Saulles Nov. 28, 1917

[108] *Who's Who in New York*, 1911, p. 348

[109] *Dark Lover*, p. 70

[110] *Dark Lover*, page 71

[111] *New York Times*, De Saulles' Friends Divorce Accusers Aug. 12, 1917

[112] *Tacoma Times*, Mrs. de Seulles [sic] Tells Her Story Nov. 26, 1917

[113] *New York Tribune*, Aug. 15, 1916

[114] *Washington Times*, Mrs. De Saulles Sails - Child Remains Here, Aug. 27, 1916

[115] *Dark Lover*, p. 70 endnotes, cite to final divorce decree, *de Saulles v. de Saulles* on file at New York City Municipal Archives

[116] NY Supplement, *in re. de Saulles*

[117] *Dark Lover*, p. 70

[118] *Washington Times*, Nov. 19, 1917

[119] *New York Tribune*, Dancing "Count" Held in Vice Raid Sep. 6, 1916

[120] *People v. Alfred Daly*, Court of General Sessions, Jan. 12, 1916

[121] *Dark Lover*, page 72

[122] *New York Times*, Prisoners Guests of Mrs. de Saulles, Nov. 30, 1917

[123] *New York Times*, Doctors Fear for Mrs. de Saulles; Begs for Her Son, Aug. 7, 1917

[124] NY Supp. p. 453, paragraph 10

[125] 1916 Trow's City Directory of New York

[126] 1905 state census of New York

[127] *Dark Lover*, page 72

[128] World War I draft registration card

[129] *New York Tribune*, De Saulles' "The Box" Sold Aug. 6, 1918

[130] photograph (1) in *El Paso Herald*, Sept. 12, 1917 and photograph (2) in *Ogden Standard*, Sept. 11, 1917, and photograph (3) in *The Evening World*, August 4, 1917

[131] *New York Times*, Insanity Defense Planned to Save Mrs. de Saulles Aug. 5, 1917

[132] *New York Times*, Mrs. de Saulles Tells Her Story of the Tragedy Aug. 6, 1917

[133] *New York Times*, Insanity Defense Planned to Save Mrs. de Saulles Aug. 5, 1917

[134] *Tacoma Times*, Nov. 23, 1917

[135] *New York Times*, Alienists Uphold Mrs. de Saulles Nov. 29, 1917

[136] *New York Times*, Mrs. de Saulles Tells Story of Husband's Neglect Nov. 27, 1917

[137] Spalding's 1904, page 93
[138] *New York Times*, Insanity Defense Planned to Save Mrs. de Saulles Aug. 5, 1917
[139] Success in Court, page 294
[140] Success in Court, page 295 - 296
[141] *New York Times*, Doctors Fear for Mrs. de Saulles; Begs for Her Son Aug. 7, 1917
[142] *New York Times, Brother Defends DeSaulles Honor* Aug. 9, 1917
[143] *New York Times, Brother Defends DeSaulles Honor* Aug. 9, 1917 (Ibid.)
[144] *New Yotk Times*, Miss Renard Plays - A Young Chilean Pianist Reappears in Aeolian Hall Oct. 14, 1917
[145] NY Supp., vol. 167, *in re. de Saulles*
[146] Solitary Dog Sculptor I, blogspot
[147] *New York Times*, John J. Graham, Ex-Surrogate, Dies Aug. 27, 1917
[148] *New York Times*, De Saulles Child Halts Murder Trial Nov. 21, 1917
[149] *New York Times*, Use Up First Panel in De Saulles Case Nov. 22, 1917
[150] *New York Times*, Defense Wins Point in De Saulles Case Nov. 23, 1917
[151] *New York Times*, Defense Wins Point in De Saulles Case Nov. 23, 1917 (Ibid.)
[152] *New York Times*, Holds De Saulles Drove Wife Mad Nov. 24, 1917
[153] *Tacoma Times*, Nov. 23, 1917
[154] *New York Times*, Holds De Saulles Drove Wife Mad Nov. 24, 1917
[155] *New York Times*, Fear Long Ordeal for Mrs. de Saulles Nov. 26, 1917
[156] *Tacoma Times*, I Danced, But Not In My Heart, Says Mrs. de Saulles Nov. 28, 1917
[157] *New York Times*, Alienists Uphold Mrs. de Saulles Nov. 29, 1917
[158] *New York Times*, Holds De Saulles Drove Wife Mad Nov. 24, 1917 (Ibid.)
[159] "Henry A. Uterhart," in <u>Success in Court</u>, ed. by Francis L. Wellman. New York, NY: The MacMillan Co. 1941. p. 297
[160] *New York Times*, I Danced, But Not In My Heart, Says Mrs. de Saulles Nov. 28, 1917
[161] *Washington Times*, De Saulles Widow is Unshaken in Story Nov. 27, 1917
[162] *Tacoma Times*, Nov. 27, 1917
[163] *New York Times*, Alienists Uphold Mrs. de Saulles Nov. 29, 1917
[164] *New York Times*, Alienists Uphold Mrs. de Saulles Nov. 29, 1917
[165] *New York Times*,Alienists Uphold Mrs. de Saulles Nov. 29, 1917
[166] *New York Times*, Prisoners Guests of Mrs. de Saulles Nov. 30, 1917
[167] *New York Times*, Prisoners Guests of Mrs. de Saulles Nov. 30, 1917
[168] *New York Times*, Says Mrs. de Saulles was Insane on Aug. 3, Dec. 1, 1917
[169] *New York Times*, Says Mrs. de Saulles was Insane on Aug. 3, Dec. 1, 1917
[170] *New York Times*, Says Mrs. de Saulles was Insane on Aug. 3, Dec. 1, 1917 (Ibid.)
[171] *New York Times*, Mrs. de Saulles is Acquitted of Husband's Murder Dec. 2, 1917
[172] *New York Times*, Mrs. de Saulles is Acquitted of Husband's Murder Dec. 2, 1917
[173] Success in Court, p. 298
[174] Success in Court, p. 281
[175] *The Independent*, Volume 92, p. 499
[176] *New York Times*, De Saulles Died in Debt 23 Dec. 1919
[177] *New York Tribune*, De Saulles' "The Box" Sold Aug. 6, 1918
[178] *New York Times*, Einstein, Ward & Co. Fail for $125,000, June 24, 1923
[179] New York City death certificate #5885
[180] Ellis Island, passenger arrival records 1909
[181] 1920 federal census, New York
[182] *Buildings*, Vol. 17
[183] Journal of San Diego History
[184] http://homepages.rootsweb.ancestry.com/~marshall/esmd6.htm
[185] St. Paul's Alumni Association, <u>St. Paul's School in the Second World War</u>, John B. Edmonds, editor. Ohrstrom Library, St. Paul's School, Concord, NH. 1950. p.142
[186] Green-wood Cemetery burial search

[187] New York Social Blue Book, 1930

[188] *New York Times*, Mrs. de Saulles in Japan March 14, 1918

[189] *New York Times*, Errazuriz, Blanca de Saulles' Brother, A Suicide in Paris Over Peggy Joyce May 2, 1922

[190] *New York Times*, Man A Mystery, Says Peggy Joyce: Actress Thinks She Might Have Prevented Errázuriz's Suicide Had She Known — Liked Him Most of All, May 3, 1922

[191] *New York Times*, Mrs. J.L. de Saulles Weds Again in Chile Dec. 23, 1921

[192] *New York Times*, Ocean Travelers Nov. 13, 1937

[193] *New York Times*, Heiress, Once Wife of J.L. de Saulles March 22, 1940

[194] *Newsweek*, April 1, 1940

[195] *Blanca Elena: Memoria Indiscreta*

[196] *The Ogden Standard*, Ogden UT, May 25, 1918

[197] *The Independent*, Volume 92, p. 499

CPSIA information can be obtained
at www.ICGtesting.com
Printed in the USA
BVHW080857171119
564073BV00019B/996/P